DOVER · THRIFT · EDITIONS

African-American Poetry

AN ANTHOLOGY: 1773–1927

EDITED BY

JOAN R. SHERMAN

DOVER PUBLICATIONS, INC.
Mineola, New York

DOVER THRIFT EDITIONS

GENERAL EDITOR: PAUL NEGRI
EDITOR OF THIS VOLUME: JOAN R. SHERMAN

Acknowledgments

"Yet Do I Marvel," "To John Keats, Poet, At Springtime" from *Color*. © 1925 by Harper & Bros., renewed 1952 by Ida Cullen; "From the Dark Tower" from *Copper Sun*. © 1927 by Harper Bros., renewed 1954 by Ida Cullen. Copyrights held by the Amistad Research Center, Tulane University, New Orleans, LA. Administered by Thompson and Thompson, New York, NY. Reprinted by permission. "Bound No'th Blues," "I, Too," "Jazzonia," "Mother to Son" from *Collected Poems*. © 1994 by the Estate of Langston Hughes. Reprinted by permission of Alfred A. Knopf Inc. "White Things," "Letter to My Sister" from J. Lee Greene, *Time's Unfading Garden: Anne Spencer's Life and Poetry*. © 1977 by Louisiana State University Press. Reprinted by permission of J. Lee Greene. "Her Lips are Copper Wire," "Georgia Dusk" from *Cane*, © 1923 by Boni & Liveright, renewed 1951 by Jean Toomer. Reprinted by permission of Liveright Publishing Corporation.

Copyright

Bibliographical Note

African-American Poetry: An Anthology: 1773–1927 is a new work, first published by Dover Publications, Inc., in 1997.

Library of Congress Cataloging-in-Publication Data

African-American poetry : an anthology, 1773–1927 / edited by Joan R. Sherman.
    p.   cm. — (Dover thrift editions)
  ISBN 0-486-29604-0 (pbk.)
  1. American poetry — Afro-American authors. 2. Afro-Americans — Poetry. I. Sherman, Joan R. II. Series.
PS591.N4A345   1997
811.008'0896073 — dc21   96-54873
                                  CIP

Manufactured in the United States of America
Dover Publications, Inc., 31 East 2nd Street, Mineola, N.Y. 11501

Note

In the nineteenth century, abolitionist and African-American periodicals printed thousands of poems by black men and women; in addition, over 150 African-Americans published one or more *volumes* of their poetry. The subjects and techniques of black poetry shifted radically in the course of the century in response to political and social events and to changing fortunes of the race. Before the Civil War, from 1830 to 1860, African-Americans wrote the finest militant race-protest poetry of the century. During Reconstruction (1866–1877), the poets responded to uncertainties about racial identity and the need for racial solidarity with sober, genteel verse. The poems of this decade either ignored race altogether or aggrandized noble black men and women for the race to emulate and white readers to welcome as responsible citizens into the larger society. In the century's last two decades, when African-Americans faced crippling discrimination, racial hostility and terrorism, their poetry became even more conservative, inspirational, descriptive, sentimental and, influenced by Booker T. Washington, accommodationist; and black poetry adhered to culturally acceptable "white" themes, techniques and ethical attitudes. From 1895 onward African-Americans also wrote dialect verse which nostalgically portrayed characters and folkways of a mythologized Southern past, charming verse that remained popular, fashionable and profitable for black poets well into the twentieth century.

Early in the new century, many black poets continued to avoid racial themes; rather, they sought "universality" and fine craftsmanship to gain approval of white audiences. Others, however, moved by the race-proud writings of W. E. B. DuBois, celebrated race consciousness in propagandistic and protest poetry or in verse that embraced "low" black folk culture and music — spirituals, jazz, ballads and blues. World War I and its aftermath engendered the outpouring of African-American creativity known as the "New Negro Renaissance" or the "Harlem Renaissance" because its center was Harlem in New York City. Many events shaped the new literature, art and music: millions of blacks emigrated from the South to cities of the North and confronted urban problems; African-Americans who served in the armed forces and encountered equality overseas changed, as Alain Locke noted, into the "new Negro" who defiantly insisted on his rights; Marcus Garvey's black nationalism inspired thousands in the early 1920s; and such periodicals as *The Crisis, The Liberator, The Messenger* and *Opportunity* welcomed poetry, fiction and essays that championed race pride and the beauty of blackness. This "Renaissance" of African-American culture flourished in the years 1917–1928 and ended with the Great Depression.

Contents

Countee Cullen

PHILLIS WHEATLEY PETERS (1753?–1784)

Brought from Africa to Boston in 1761, the young slave became well-educated and in 1773 published *Poems on Various Subjects, Religious and Moral*.

ON BEING BROUGHT FROM AFRICA TO AMERICA

'Twas mercy brought me from my pagan land,
Taught my benighted soul to understand
That there's a God, that there's a Savior too:
Once I redemption neither sought nor knew.
Some view our sable race with scornful eye,
"Their color is a diabolic dye."
Remember, Christians, Negroes, black as Cain,
May be refin'd, and join th' angelic train.

AN HYMN TO THE EVENING

Soon as the sun forsook the eastern main
The pealing thunder shook the heav'nly plain;
Majestic grandeur! From the zephyr's wing,
Exhales the incense of the blooming spring.
Soft purl the streams, the birds renew their notes,
And through the air their mingled music floats.

Through all the heav'ns what beauteous dyes are
    spread!
But the west glories in the deepest red:
So may our breasts with ev'ry virtue glow,
The living temples of our God below!

Fill'd with the praise of him who gives the light,
And draws the sable curtains of the night,
Let placid slumbers soothe each weary mind,
At morn to wake more heav'nly, more refin'd;

So shall the labors of the day begin
More pure, more guarded from the snares of sin.

Night's leaden sceptre seals my drowsy eyes,
Then cease, my song, till fair Aurora rise.

GEORGE MOSES HORTON (1797?–1883?)

A slave in North Carolina for 66 years, Horton published 150 poems in three volumes from 1829 to 1865. His subjects include his bondage, love, religion, nature, the art of poetry and the Civil War.

LIBERTY AND SLAVERY

Alas! and am I born for this,
   To wear this slavish chain?
Deprived of all created bliss,
   Through hardship, toil and pain!

How long have I in bondage lain,
   And languished to be free!
Alas! and must I still complain —
   Deprived of liberty.

Oh, Heaven! and is there no relief
   This side the silent grave —
To soothe the pain — to quell the grief
   And anguish of a slave?

Come Liberty, thou cheerful sound,
   Roll through my ravished ears!
Come, let my grief in joys be drowned,
   And drive away my fears.

Say unto foul oppression, Cease:
   Ye tyrants rage no more,
And let the joyful trump of peace,
   Now bid the vassal soar.

Soar on the pinions of that dove
   Which long has cooed for thee,
And breathed her notes from Afric's grove,
   The sound of Liberty.

Oh, Liberty! thou golden prize,
   So often sought by blood —
We crave thy sacred sun to rise,
   The gift of nature's God!

Bid Slavery hide her haggard face,
   And barbarism fly:
I scorn to see the sad disgrace
   In which enslaved I lie.

Dear Liberty! upon thy breast,
   I languish to respire;
And like the Swan unto her nest,
   I'd to thy smiles retire.

Oh, blest asylum — heavenly balm!
   Unto thy boughs I flee —
And in thy shades the storm shall calm,
   With songs of Liberty!

EARLY AFFECTION

I lov'd thee from the earliest dawn,
   When first I saw thy beauty's ray,
And will, until life's eve comes on,
   And beauty's blossom fades away;
And when all things go well with thee,
With smiles and tears remember me.

I'll love thee when thy morn is past,
   And wheedling gallantry is o'er,
When youth is lost in ages blast,
   And beauty can ascend no more,
And when life's journey ends with thee,
O, then look back and think of me.

I'll love thee with a smile or frown,
   'Mid sorrow's gloom or pleasure's light,
And when the chain of life runs down,
   Pursue thy last eternal flight,
When thou hast spread thy wing to flee,
Still, still, a moment wait for me.

I'll love thee for those sparkling eyes,
   To which my fondness was betray'd,
Bearing the tincture of the skies,

To glow when other beauties fade,
   And when they sink too low to see,
   Reflect an azure beam on me.

TROUBLED WITH THE ITCH AND RUBBING WITH SULPHUR

'Tis bitter, yet 'tis sweet;
    Scratching effects but transient ease;
Pleasure and pain together meet
    And vanish as they please.

My nails, the only balm,
    To every bump are oft applied,
And thus the rage will sweetly calm
    Which aggravates my hide.

It soon returns again:
    A frown succeeds to every smile;
Grinning I scratch and curse the pain
    But grieve to be so vile.

In fine, I know not which
    Can play the most deceitful game:
The devil, sulphur, or the itch.
    The three are but the same.

The devil sows the itch,
    And sulphur has a loathsome smell,
And with my clothes as black as pitch
    I stink where'er I dwell.

Excoriated deep,
    By friction played on every part,
It oft deprives me of my sleep
    And plagues me to my heart.

IMPLORING TO BE RESIGNED AT DEATH

Let me die and not tremble at death,
    But smile at the close of my day,
And then at the flight of my breath,
    Like a bird of the morning in May,
       Go chanting away.

Let me die without fear of the dead,
    No horrors my soul shall dismay,
And with faith's pillow under my head,
    With defiance to mortal decay,
            Go chanting away.

Let me die like a son of the brave,
    And martial distinction display;
Nor shrink from a thought of the grave,
    No, but with a smile from the clay,
            Go chanting away.

Let me die glad, regardless of pain,
    No pang to this world betray,
And the spirit cut loose from its chains,
    So loath in the flesh to delay,
            Go chanting away.

Let me die, and my worst foe forgive,
    When death veils the last vital ray;
Since I have but a moment to live,
    Let me, when the last debt I pay,
            Go chanting away.

GEORGE MOSES HORTON, MYSELF

I feel myself in need
    Of the inspiring strains of ancient lore,
My heart to lift, my empty mind to feed,
    And all the world explore.

I know that I am old
    And never can recover what is past,
But for the future may some light unfold
    And soar from ages blast.

I feel resolved to try,
    My wish to prove, my calling to pursue,
Or mount up from the earth into the sky,
    To show what Heaven can do.

My genius from a boy,
    Has fluttered like a bird within my heart;
But could not thus confined her powers employ,
    Impatient to depart.

She like a restless bird,
Would spread her wings, her power to be unfurl'd,
And let her songs be loudly heard,
And dart from world to world.

JOSHUA McCARTER SIMPSON (1820?–1876)

Simpson's satirical protest poems clamored for emancipation and civil rights. They were set to popular tunes, and fugitives on the Underground Railroad sang Simpson's song-poems in the 1850s.

AWAY TO CANADA

Air — *"O Susannah"*
Adapted to the case of Mr. S., Fugitive from Tennessee.

I'm on my way to Canada,
That cold and dreary land;
The dire effects of slavery,
I can no longer stand.
My soul is vexed within me so,
To think that I'm a slave;
I've now resolved to strike the blow
For freedom or the grave.

O righteous Father,
Wilt thou not pity me?
And aid me on to Canada,
Where colored men are free.

I heard Victoria plainly say,
If we would all forsake
Our native land of slavery,
And come across the Lake.
That she was standing on the shore,
With arms extended wide,
To give us all a peaceful home,
Beyond the rolling tide.

Farewell, old master!
That's enough for me —

I'm going straight to Canada,
    Where colored men are free.

* * *

I heard old master pray last night —
    I heard him pray for me;
That God would come, and in his might
    From Satan set me free;
So I from Satan would escape,
    And flee the wrath to come —
If there's a fiend in human shape,
    Old master must be one.

        O! old master,
            While you pray for me,
        I'm doing all I can to reach
            The land of Liberty.

Ohio's not the place for me;
    For I was much surprised,
So many of her sons to see
    In garments of disguise.
Her name has gone out through the world,
    Free Labor, Soil, and Men;
But slaves had better far be hurled
    Into the Lion's Den.

        Farewell, Ohio!
            I am not safe in thee;
        I'll travel on to Canada,
            Where colored men are free.

I've now embarked for yonder shore,
    Where man's a *man by law*,
The vessel soon will bear me o'er,
    To shake the Lion's paw.
I no more dread the Auctioneer,
    Nor fear the master's frowns,
I no more tremble when I hear
    The beying negro-hounds.

        O! old Master,
            Don't think hard of me —
        I'm just in sight of Canada,
            Where colored men are free.

I've landed safe upon the shore,
　Both soul and body free;
My blood and brain, and tears no more
　Will drench old Tennessee.
But I behold the scalding tear,
　Now stealing from my eye,
To think my wife — my only dear,
　A slave must live and die.

　　O, Susannah!
　　　Don't grieve after me —
　　For ever at a throne of grace,
　　　I will remember thee.

TO THE WHITE PEOPLE OF AMERICA

Air — "Massa's in the Cold, Cold Ground"

O'er this wide extended country,
　Hear the solemn echoes roll,
For a long and weary century,
　Those cries have gone from pole to pole;
See the white man sway his sceptre,
　In *one* hand he holds the rod —
In the *other* hand the Scripture,
　And says that he's a man of God.

　　Hear ye that mourning?
　　　'Tis your brothers' cry!
　　O! ye wicked men take warning,
　　　The day will come when you must die.

Lo! Ten thousand steeples shining
　Through this mighty Christian land,
While four millions slaves all pining
　And dying 'neath the Tyrant's hand.
See the *"blood-stained"* Christian banner
　Followed by a host of saints (?)
While they loudly sing Hosannah,
　We hear the dying slave's complaints:

　　Hear ye that mourning?
　　　Anglo-sons of God,
　　O! ye Hypocrites take warning,
　　　And shun your sable brothers blood.

In our Legislative members,
    Few there are with humane souls,
Though they speak in tones of thunder
    'Gainst sins which they cannot control,
Women's rights and annexation,
    Is the topic by the way,
While poor Africa's sable nation
    For mercy, cry both by night and day.

        Hear ye that mourning?
        'Tis a solemn sound,
        O! ye wicked men take warning,
        For God will send his judgment down.

Tell us not of distant Island —
    Never will we colonize:
Send us not to British Highlands,
    For this is neither just nor wise,
Give us equal rights and chances,
    All the rights of citizens —
And as light and truth advances,
    We'll show you that we all are men.

        Hear ye that mourning?
        'Tis your brothers sigh,
        O! ye wicked men take warning,
        The judgment day will come by and by.

JAMES MONROE WHITFIELD (1822–1871)

Whitfield was a barber by trade, a major propagandist for black separatism and racial justice, and an outstanding poet whose impassioned protest verse masterfully combined bitter anger and artistry.

HOW LONG?

    How long, O gracious God! how long,
        Shall power lord it over right?
    The feeble, trampled by the strong,
        Remain in slavery's gloomy night?
    In every region of the earth,
        Oppression rules with iron power;
    And every man of sterling worth,

Whose soul disdains to cringe or cower
Beneath a haughty tyrant's nod,
And, supplicating, kiss the rod
That, wielded by oppression's might,
Smites to the earth his dearest right, —
The right to speak, and think, and feel,
    And spread his uttered thoughts abroad,
To labor for the common weal,
    Responsible to none but God, —
Is threatened with the dungeon's gloom,
The felon's cell, the traitor's doom,
And treacherous politicians league
    With hireling priests, to crush and ban
All who expose their vile intrigue,
    And vindicate the rights of man.
How long shall Afric' raise to thee
    Her fettered hand, O Lord! in vain,
And plead in fearful agony
    For vengeance for her children slain?
I see the Gambia's swelling flood,
    And Niger's darkly rolling wave,
Bear on their bosoms, stained with blood,
    The bound and lacerated slave;
While numerous tribes spread near and far,
Fierce, devastating, barbarous war,
Earth's fairest scenes in ruin laid,
To furnish victims for that trade,
Which breeds on earth such deeds of shame,
As fiends might blush to hear or name.

                *   *   *

The same unholy sacrifice
Where'er I turn bursts on mine eyes,
Of princely pomp, and priestly pride,
    The people trampled in the dust,
Their dearest, holiest rights denied,
    Their hopes destroyed, their spirit crushed:
But when I turn the land to view,
    Which claims, par excellence, to be
The refuge of the brave and true,
    The strongest bulwark of the free,
The grand asylum for the poor
    And trodden down of every land,

Where they may rest in peace, secure,
  Nor fear the oppressor's iron hand, —
Worse scenes of rapine, lust, and shame,
Than e'er disgraced the Russian name,
Worse than the Austrian ever saw,
Are sanctioned here as righteous law.
Here might the Austrian butcher make
  Progress in shameful cruelty,
Where women-whippers proudly take
  The meed and praise of chivalry.
Here might the cunning Jesuit learn,
  Though skilled in subtle sophistry,
And trained to persevere in stern
  Unsympathizing cruelty,
And call that good, which, right or wrong,
Will tend to make his order strong:
He here might learn from those who stand
  High in the gospel ministry,
The very magnates of the land
  In evangelic piety,
That conscience must not only bend
  To everything the church decrees,
But it must also condescend,
  When drunken politicians please
To place their own inhuman acts
  Above the "higher law" of God,
And on the hunted victim's tracks
  Cheer the malignant fiends of blood,
To help the man-thief bind the chain
  Upon his Christian brother's limb,
And bear to slavery's hell again
  The bound and suffering child of Him
Who died upon the cross, to save
Alike, the master and the slave.
While all the oppressed from every land
Are welcomed here with open hand,
And fulsome praises rend the heaven
For those who have the fetters riven
Of European tyranny,
And bravely struck for liberty;
And while from thirty thousand fanes
  Mock prayers go up, and hymns are sung,
Three million drag their clanking chains,
  "Unwept, unhonored, and unsung:"

Doomed to a state of slavery,
   Compared with which the darkest night
Of European tyranny,
   Seems brilliant as the noonday light.
While politicians void of shame,
   Cry this is law and liberty,
The clergy lend the awful name
   And sanction of the Deity,
To help sustain the monstrous wrong,
And crush the weak beneath the strong.

             *   *   *

Yet to the eye of him who reads
   The fate of nations past and gone,
And marks with care the wrongful deeds
   By which their power was overthrown, —
Worse plagues than Egypt ever felt
   Are seen wide-spreading through the land,
Announcing that the heinous guilt
   On which the nation proudly stands,
Has risen to Jehovah's throne,
   And kindled his Almighty ire,
And broadcast through the land has sown
   The seeds of a devouring fire;
Blasting with foul pestiferous breath
   The fountain springs of mortal life,
And planting deep the seeds of death,
   And future germs of deadly strife;
And moral darkness spreads its gloom
   Over the land in every part,
And buries in a living tomb
   Each generous prompting of the heart.

             *   *   *

How long, O Lord! shall such vile deeds
   Be acted in thy holy name,
And senseless bigots o'er their creeds
   Fill the whole world with war and flame?
How long shall ruthless tyrants claim
   Thy sanction to their bloody laws,
And throw the mantle of thy name
   Around their foul, unhallowed cause?

How long shall all the people bow
   As vassals of the favored few,
And shame the pride of manhood's brow, —
   Give what to God alone is due,
Homage to wealth and rank and power,
Vain shadows of a passing hour?
Oh, for a pen of living fire,
   A tongue of flame, an arm of steel!
To rouse the people's slumbering ire,
   And teach the tyrants' hearts to feel.
O Lord! in vengeance now appear.
   And guide the battles for the right,
The spirits of the fainting cheer,
   And nerve the patriot's arm with might;
Till slavery's banished from the world,
And tyrants from their power hurled;
And all mankind, from bondage free,
Exult in glorious liberty.

THE MISANTHROPIST

In vain thou bid'st me strike the lyre,
   And sing a song of mirth and glee,
Or kindling with poetic fire,
   Attempt some higher minstrelsy;
In vain, in vain! for every thought
   That issues from this throbbing brain,
Is from its first conception fraught
With gloom and darkness, woe and pain.
From earliest youth my path has been
   Cast in life's darkest, deepest shade,
Where no bright ray did intervene,
   Nor e'er a passing sunbeam strayed;
But all was dark and cheerless night,
   Without one ray of hopeful light.
From childhood, then, through many a shock,
   I've battled with the ills of life,
Till, like a rude and rugged rock,
   My heart grew callous in the strife.
When other children passed the hours
   In mirth, and play, and childish glee,
Or gathering the summer flowers
   By gentle brook, or flowery lea,
I sought the wild and rugged glen

Where Nature, in her sternest mood,
Far from the busy haunts of men,
  Frowned in the darksome solitude.
There have I mused till gloomy night,
  Like the death-angel's brooding wing,
Would shut out everything from sight,
  And o'er the scene her mantle fling;
And seeking then my lonely bed
  To pass the night in sweet repose,
Around my fevered, burning head,
  Dark visions of the night arose;
And the stern scenes which day had viewed
  In sterner aspects rose before me,
And specters of still sterner mood
  Waved their menacing fingers o'er me.
When the dark storm-fiend soared abroad,
  And swept to earth the waving grain,
On whirlwind through the forest rode,
  And stirred to foam the heaving main,
I loved to mark the lightning's flash,
  And listen to the ocean's roar,
Or hear the pealing thunder's crash,
  And see the mountain torrents pour
Down precipices dark and steep,
  Still bearing, in their headlong course
To meet th' embrace of ocean deep,
  Mementoes of the tempest's force;
For fire and tempest, flood and storm,
  Wakened deep echoes in my soul,
And made the quickening life-blood warm
  With impulse that knew no control;
And the fierce lightning's lurid flash
  Rending the somber clouds asunder,
Followed by the terrific crash
  Which marks the hoarsely rattling thunder,
Seemed like the gleams of lurid light
  Which flashed across my seething brain,
Succeeded by a darker night,
  With wilder horrors in its train.

                *   *   *

Whene'er I turned in gentler mood
  To scan the old historic page,

It was not where the wise and good,
    The Bard, the Statesman, or the Sage,
Had drawn in lines of living light,
Lessons of virtue, truth and right;
But that which told of secret league,
    Where deep conspiracies were rife,
And where, through foul and dark intrigue,
    Were sowed the seeds of deadly strife;
Where hostile armies met to seal
    Their country's doom, for woe or weal;
Where the grim-visaged death-fiend drank
    His full supply of human gore,
And poured through every hostile rank
    The tide of battle's awful roar;
For then my spirit seemed to soar
    Away to where such scenes were rife,
And high above the battle's roar
    Sit as spectator of the strife —
And in those scenes of war and woe,
A fierce and fitful pleasure know.

                *   *   *

There was a time that I did love,
    Such love as those alone can know,
Whose blood like burning lava moves,
    Whose passions like the lightning glow;
And when that ardent, truthful love,
    Was blighted in its opening bloom,
And all around, below, above,
    Seemed like the darkness of the tomb,
'Twas then my stern and callous heart,
Riven in its most vital part
Seemed like some gnarled and knotted oak,
That, shivered by the lightning's stroke,
Stands in the lonely wanderer's path,
A ghastly monument of wrath.
Then how can I attune the lyre
    To strains of love or joyous glee?
Break forth in patriotic fire,
    Or soar on higher minstrelsy,
To sing the praise of virtue bright,
Condemn the wrong, and laud the right;
When neither vice nor guilt can fling

A darker shadow o'er my breast,
Nor even Virtue's self can bring,
   Unto my moody spirit, rest.
It may not be, it cannot be!
   Let others strike the sounding string,
And in rich strains of harmony,
   Songs of poetic beauty sing;
But mine must still the portion be,
   However dark and drear the doom,
To live estranged from sympathy,
   Buried in doubt, despair and gloom;
To bare my breast to every blow,
To know no friend, and fear no foe,
Each generous impulse trod to dust,
Each noble aspiration crushed,
Each feeling struck with withering blight,
With no regard for wrong or right,
No fear of hell, no hope of heaven,
Die all unwept and unforgiven,
Content to know and dare the worst
Which mankind's hate, and heaven's curse,
Can heap upon my living head,
Or cast around my memory dead;
And let them on my tombstone trace,
Here lies the Pariah of his race.

FRANCES ELLEN WATKINS HARPER (1824–1911)

Harper earned financial independence and nationwide acclaim with her poetry, essays, fiction and public readings and lectures on behalf of racial equality, women's and children's rights, Christian morality and temperance.

BURY ME IN A FREE LAND

Make me a grave where'er you will,
In a lowly plain, or a lofty hill,
Make it among earth's humblest graves,
But not in a land where men are slaves.

I could not rest if around my grave
I heard the steps of a trembling slave:

His shadow above my silent tomb
Would make it a place of fearful gloom.

I could not rest if I heard the tread
Of a coffle gang to the shambles led,
And the mother's shriek of wild despair
Rise like a curse on the trembling air.

I could not sleep if I saw the lash
Drinking her blood at each fearful gash,
And I saw her babes torn from her breast,
Like trembling doves from their parent nest.

I'd shudder and start if I heard the bay
Of blood-hounds seizing their human prey,
And I heard the captive plead in vain
As they bound afresh his galling chain.

If I saw young girls from their mother's arms
Bartered and sold for their youthful charms,
My eye would flash with a mournful flame,
My death-paled cheek grow red with shame.

I would sleep, dear friends, where bloated might
Can rob no man of his dearest right;
My rest shall be calm in any grave
Where none can call his brother a slave.

I ask no monument, proud and high
To arrest the gaze of the passers-by;
All that my yearning spirit craves,
Is bury me not in a land of slaves.

TO THE UNION SAVERS OF CLEVELAND

Men of Cleveland, had a vulture
    Sought a timid dove for prey,
Would you not, with human pity,
    Drive the gory bird away?

Had you seen a feeble lambkin,
    Shrinking from a wolf so bold,
Would ye not to shield the trembler,
    In your arms have made its fold?

But when she, a hunted sister,
    Stretched her hands that ye might save,

Colder far than Zembla's regions
    Was the answer that ye gave.

On the Union's bloody altar,
    Was your hapless victim laid;
Mercy, truth and justice shuddered,
    But your hands would give no aid.

And ye sent her back to torture,
    Robbed of freedom and of right.
Thrust the wretched, captive stranger,
    Back to slavery's gloomy night.

Back where brutal men may trample,
    On her honor and her fame;
And unto her lips so dusky,
    Press the cup of woe and shame.

There is blood upon your city,
    Dark and dismal is the stain;
And your hands would fail to cleanse it,
    Though Lake Erie ye should drain.

There's a curse upon your Union,
    Fearful sounds are in the air;
As if thunderbolts were framing,
    Answers to the bondsman's prayer.

Ye may offer human victims,
    Like the heathen priests of old;
And may barter manly honor
    For the Union and for gold.

But ye can not stay the whirlwind,
    When the storm begins to break;
And our God doth rise in judgment,
    For the poor and needy's sake.

And, your sin-cursed, guilty Union,
    Shall be shaken to its base,
Till ye learn that simple justice,
    Is the right of every race.

FROM MOSES: A STORY OF THE NILE

Moses sought again the presence of the king:
And Pharaoh's brow grew dark with wrath,
And rising up in angry haste, he said
Defiantly, "If thy God be great, show
Us some sign or token of his power."
Then Moses threw his rod upon the floor,
And it trembled with a sign of life;
The dark wood glowed, then changed into a thing
Of glistening scales and golden rings, and green
And brown and purple stripes; a hissing, hateful
Thing, that glared its fiery eye, and darting forth
From Moses' side, lay coiled and panting
At the monarch's feet. With wonder open-eyed
The king gazed on the changed rod, then called
For his magicians — wily men, well versed
In sinful lore — and bade them do the same.
And they, leagued with the powers of night, did
Also change their rods to serpents; then Moses'
Serpent darted forth, and with a startling hiss
And angry gulp, he swallowed the living things
That coiled along his path. And thus did Moses
Show that Israel's God had greater power
Than those dark sons of night.
                        But not by this alone
Did God his mighty power reveal: He changed
Their waters; every fountain, well and pool
Was red with blood, and lips, all parched with thirst,
Shrank back in horror from the crimson draughts.
And then the worshiped Nile grew full of life:
Millions of frogs swarmed from the stream — they clogged
The pathway of the priests and filled the sacred
Fanes, and crowded into Pharaoh's bed, and hopped
Into his trays of bread, and slumbered in his
Ovens and his pans.

There came another plague, of loathsome vermin;
They were gray and creeping things, that made
Their very clothes alive with dark and sombre
Spots — things of loathsome in the land, they did
Suspend the service of the temple; for no priest
Dared to lift his hand to any god with one
Of those upon him. And then the sky grew
Dark, as if a cloud were passing o'er its

Changeless blue; a buzzing sound broke o'er
The city, and the land was swarmed with flies.
The Murrain laid their cattle low; the hail
Cut off the first fruits of the Nile; the locusts
With their hungry jaws, destroyed the later crops,
And left the ground as brown and bare as if a fire
Had scorched it through.
                          Then angry blains
And fiery boils did blur the flesh of man
And beast; and then for three long days, nor saffron
Tint, nor crimson flush, nor soft and silvery light
Divided day from morn, nor told the passage
Of the hours; men rose not from their seats, but sat
In silent awe. That lengthened night lay like a burden
On the air, — a darkness one might almost gather
In his hand, it was so gross and thick. Then came
The last dread plague — the death of the first born.

           *   *   *

"SIR, WE WOULD SEE JESUS"

We would see Jesus; earth is grand,
Flowing out from her Creator's hand.
Like one who tracks his steps with light,
His footsteps ever greet our sight;
The earth below, the sky above,
Are full of tokens of his love;
But 'mid the fairest scenes we've sighed —
Our hearts are still unsatisfied.

We would see Jesus; proud and high
Temples and domes have met our eye.
We've gazed upon the glorious thought,
By earnest hands in marble wrought,
And listened where the flying feet
Beat time to music, soft and sweet;
But bow'rs of ease, and halls of pride,
Our yearning hearts ne'er satisfied.

We would see Jesus; we have heard
Tidings our inmost souls have stirred,
How, from their chambers full of night,
The darkened eyes receive the light;

How, at the music of his voice,
The lame do leap, the dumb rejoice.
Anxious we'll wait until we've seen
The good and gracious Nazarene.

LEARNING TO READ

Very soon the Yankee teachers
   Came down and set up school;
But, oh! how the Rebs did hate it, —
   It was agin' their rule.

Our masters always tried to hide
   Book learning from our eyes;
Knowledge did'nt agree with slavery —
   'Twould make us all too wise.

But some of us would try to steal
   A little from the book,
And put the words together,
   And learn by hook or crook.

I remember Uncle Caldwell,
   Who took pot liquor fat
And greased the pages of his book,
   And hid it in his hat.

And had his master ever seen
   The leaves upon his head,
He'd have thought them greasy papers,
   But nothing to be read.

And there was Mr. Turner's Ben,
   Who heard the children spell,
And picked the words right up by heart,
   And learned to read 'em well.

Well, the Northern folks kept sending
   The Yankee teachers down;
And they stood right up and helped us,
   Though Rebs did sneer and frown.

And I longed to read my Bible,
   For precious words it said;
But when I begun to learn it,
   Folks just shook their heads,

And said there is no use trying,
   Oh! Chloe, you're too late;
But as I was rising sixty,
   I had no time to wait.

So I got a pair of glasses,
   And straight to work I went,
And never stopped till I could read
   The hymns and Testament.

Then I got a little cabin
   A place to call my own —
And I felt as independent
   As the queen upon her throne.

SONGS FOR THE PEOPLE

Let me make the songs for the people,
   Songs for the old and young;
Songs to stir like a battle-cry
   Wherever they are sung.

Not for the clashing of sabres,
   Nor carnage nor for strife;
But songs to thrill the hearts of men
   With more abundant life.

Let me make the songs for the weary,
   Amid life's fever and fret,
Till hearts shall relax their tension,
   And careworn brows forget.

Let me sing for little children,
   Before their footsteps stray,
Sweet anthems of love and duty,
   To float o'er life's highway.

I would sing for the poor and aged,
   When shadows dim their sight;
Of the bright and restful mansions,
   Where there shall be no night.

Our world, so worn and weary,
   Needs music, pure and strong,
To hush the jangle and discords
   Of sorrow, pain, and wrong.

> Music to soothe all its sorrow,
>   Till war and crime shall cease;
> And the hearts of men grown tender
>   Girdle the world with peace.

JAMES MADISON BELL (1826–1902)

A plasterer from Ohio, for 40 years Bell wrote, published and gave public readings of his orations in verse. He also lectured nationwide for abolitionism and black educational and legal rights.

FROM A POEM ENTITLED THE DAY AND THE WAR

> Though Tennyson, the poet king,
>   Has sung of Balaklava's charge,
> Until his thund'ring cannons ring
>   From England's center to her marge,
> The pleasing duty still remains
> To sing a people from their chains —
> To sing what none have yet assay'd,
> The wonders of the Black Brigade.
> The war had raged some twenty moons,
> Ere they in columns or platoons,
> To win them censure or applause,
> Were marshal'd in the Union cause —
> Prejudged of slavish cowardice,
> While many a taunt and foul device
> Came weekly forth with Harper's sheet,
> To feed that base, infernal cheat.
>
> But how they would themselves demean,
> Has since most gloriously been seen.
> 'Twas seen at Milliken's dread bend!
> Where e'en the Furies seemed to lend
> To dark Secession all their aid,
> To crush the Union Black Brigade.
>
> The war waxed hot, and bullets flew
>   Like San Francisco's summer sand,
> But they were there to dare and do,
>   E'en to the last, to save the land.

And when the leaders of their corps
   Grew wild with fear, and quit the field,
The dark remembrance of their scars
   Before them rose, they could not yield:
And, sounding o'er the battle din,
   They heard their standard-bearer cry —
"Rally! and prove that ye are men!
   Rally! and let us do or die!
For war, nor death, shall boast a shade
   To daunt the Union Black Brigade!"

And thus he played the hero's part,
   Till on the ramparts of the foe
A score of bullets pierced his heart,
   He sank within the trench below.
His comrades saw, and fired with rage,
Each sought his man, him to engage
In single combat. Ah! 'twas then
The Black Brigade proved they were men!
For ne'er did Swiss! or Russ! or knight!
   Against such fearful odds arrayed,
With more persistent valor fight,
   Than did the Union Black Brigade!

As five to one, so stood their foes,
When that defiant shout arose,
And 'long their closing columns ran,
Commanding each to choose his man!
And ere the sound had died away,
Full many a ranting rebel lay
Gasping piteously for breath —
Struggling with the pangs of death,
From bayonet thrust or shining blade,
Plunged to the hilt by the Black Brigade.
   And thus they fought, and won a name —
None brighter on the scroll of Fame;
For out of one full corps of men,
But one remained unwounded, when
The dreadful fray had fully past —
All killed or wounded but the last!

   And though they fell, as has been seen,
Each slept his lifeless foes between,
And marked the course and paved the way
To ushering in a better day.
Let Balaklava's cannons roar,

And Tennyson his hosts parade,
But ne'er was seen and never more
    The equals of the Black Brigade!

Then nerve thy heart, gird on thy sword,
For dark Oppression's ruthless horde
And thy tried friends are in the field —
Say which shall triumph, which shall yield?
Shall they that heed not man nor God —
Vile monsters of the *gory rod* —
Dark forgers of the *rack* and *chain*:
Shall *they* prevail — and Thraldom's reign,
With all his dark unnumber'd ills,
Become eternal as the hills?
No! by the blood of freemen slain,
On hot-contested field and main,
And by the mingled sweat and tears,
Extorted through these many years
From Afric's patient sons of toil —
Weak victims of a braggart's spoil —
This bastard plant, the Upas tree,
Shall not supplant our liberty!

FROM AN ANNIVERSARY POEM ENTITLED THE PROGRESS OF LIBERTY

Though slavery's dead, yet there remains
A work for those from whom the chains
Today are falling one by one;
Nor should they deem their labor done,
Nor shrink the task, however hard,
While it insures a great reward,
And bids them on its might depend
For perfect freedom in the end.

Commend yourselves through self-respect;
    Let self-respect become your guide:
Then will consistency reflect
    Your rightful claims to manhood's pride.
But while you cringe and basely cower,
    And while you ostracise your class,
Heaven will ne'er assume the power
    To elevate you as a mass.

In this yourselves must take the lead;
   You must yourselves first elevate;
Till then the world will ne'er concede
   Your claims to manhood's high estate.
Respect yourself; this forms the base
   Of manhood's claim to man's regard.
Next to yourself, respect your race,
   Whose care should be your constant ward;
Remember that you are a class
   Distinct and separate in this land,
And all the wealth you may amass,
   Or skill, or learning, won't command
That high respect you vainly seek,
   Until you practice what you claim —
Until the acts and words you speak
   Shall, in the concrete, be the same.

Screen not behind a pallid brow;
   Paint lends no virtue to the face;
Until the Black's respected, thou,
   With all the branches of his race,
Must bow beneath the cruel ban
   And often feel the wrinkled brow
Bent on you by a fellow-man
   Not half so worthy, oft, as thou.

Away with caste, and let us fight
   As men, the battles of the free,
And Heaven will arm you with the might
   And power of man's divinity.
There may be causes for distrust,
And many an act that seems unjust;
But who, when taking all in all,
   And summing up our present state,
Would find no objects to extol,
   No worthy deeds to emulate?

CHARLOTTE L. FORTEN GRIMKÉ (1837–1914)

Born into the leading African-American family of Philadelphia, Grimké joined in antislavery activities, taught freed slaves in South Carolina and published some fine poetry, essays and a journal.

WORDSWORTH

Poet of the serene and thoughtful lay!
In youth's fair dawn, when the soul, still untried,
Longs for life's conflict, and seeks restlessly
Food for its cravings in the stirring songs,
The thrilling strains of more impassioned bards;
Or, eager for fresh joys, culls with delight
The flowers that bloom in fancy's fairy realm —
We may not prize the mild and steadfast ray
That streams from thy pure soul in tranquil song
But, in our riper years, when through the heat
And burden of the day we struggle on,
Breasting the stream upon whose shores we dreamed,
Weary of all the turmoil and the din
Which drowns the finer voices of the soul;
We turn to thee, true priest of Nature's fane,
And find the rest our fainting spirits need, —
The calm, more ardent singers cannot give;
As in the glare intense of tropic days,
Gladly we turn from the sun's radiant beams,
And grateful hail fair Luna's tender light.

ALFRED ISLAY WALDEN (1847?–1884)

After 18 years of slavery in North Carolina, Walden overcame destitution and blindness to earn a teaching degree at Howard University and ordination as a minister.

WISH FOR AN OVERCOAT

Oh! had I now an overcoat,
    For I am nearly freezing;
My head and lungs are stopped with cold,
    And often I am sneezing.

And, too, while passing through the street,
    Where merchants all are greeting,
They say, young man this is the coat
    That you should wear to meeting.

Then, looking down upon my feet,
    For there my boots are bursting,
With upturned heels and grinning toes,
    With tacks which long were rusting.

Ah! how they view my doeskin pants
    With long and crooked stitches,
They say, young man would you not like
    To have some other breeches?

My head is also hatless too,
    The wind is swiftly blowing,
They say, young man will you not freeze?
    See ye not how it's snowing?

And now they take me by the hand,
    And lead me toward the store,
And some are pulling down the coats
    Before I reach the door.

So walk I in, their goods to price,
    To quench a thirst that's burning,
And freely would I buy a coat,
    But nothing I am earning.

They say to me, I should have known,
    That winter time was coming,
When I was roaming through the park,
    With birds around me humming.

Their logic's true, I must confess,
    And all they say is pleasant;
But did I know that I would have
    No overcoat at present?

To satisfy these craving Jews,
    To buy I am not able,
For it is more than I can do
    To meet my wants at table.

Therefore my skin will toughly grow,
    Will grant to me this favor,
That I may learn to stand as much
    As little Jack, the sailor.

And if I live till winter's passed,
    Though nature's harps unstringing,
I then will fly to yon woodland
    To hear the oak trees singing.

Then I will not on hero's fame,
    Ride swiftly on to victory,
Although my saddle may be made
    Of cotton sacks or hickory.

But if I die, farewell to all,
    Oh! who will tell the story,
That I have lived a noble life
    And now gone home to glory?

Yes, who will chant a song of praise
    For me — who will be weeping —
When I have yielded to the grave,
    And 'mid the dead am sleeping?

But some will ask, "how did he die?
    It was without my knowing;
Was it because he caught a cold,
    Last year when it was snowing?"

The answer now comes hurling back,
    In words I cannot utter,
It was not by a cold alone,
    But partly bread and butter.

[This poem is dedicated to my own necessities and wants.]

ALBERRY ALSTON WHITMAN (1851–1901)

The "Poet Laureate of the Negro Race" was born a slave and became the finest African-American poet of his age. His epic-length Romantic poems reveal superior skills with a great variety of moods, subjects, emotions and techniques.

FROM NOT A MAN, AND YET A MAN

* * *

The hunters mount menacing as they go,
And thro' the village disappearing slow,
Betake them to the woods and brisker ride
Along the neighb'ring forest's eastern side.

There where a peaceful streamlet ambles by
Thro' dabbling ferns and gossips cheerfully
With shaggy roots that reach into the flood,
They spy a maid just bord'ring womanhood.
Now ranging feathers in her head-gear fair,
And with her fingers combing out her hair,
She on the prone bank stands, where smoothly flows
The liquid mirror, and her beauty shows.
Now grand old sylvans raise their solemn heads,
And make obesience as she lightly treads
Beneath their outstretched arms, and looks around
To gather nuts upon the leaf-spread ground.
The hunters see her, wayward, wild and sweet;
She sees them not, nor hears their horses' feet.
"Hold!" cries Sir Maxey, "What a lovely maid!
Ah! what a princess of this ancient shade!
Let me behold her! Quiet! Don't move!
Did admiration e'er see such a dove?
Young love no sweeter image ever drew
Upon imagination's tender view.
Her perfect form in idle movements seems
The fleeting creature of our youthful dreams."
A rougher comrade at his elbow growls,
"A purty good 'un o' the dusky fowls,
She's hard o' hearin', le'me try my gun;
Give her a skere, and see the red wench run."
His deadly eye directs, his rifle speaks,

The maiden throws her arms and runs and shrieks;
Towards the hunters pitiously flies,
The mournful wastes lamenting with her cries,
Till at their feet she sinks, and all is o'er,
Poor bleeding Nanawawa is no more.

*   *   *

Thrice hail! proud land, whose genius boasts a Clay!
The Cicero of slavery's palmy day,
The gifted champion of Compromise,
Whose mien majestic filled a nation's eyes;
And on the eloquence of whose wise tongue
A learned Senate in rapt silence hung;
A Senate, too, whose fame no one impugns,
Of Websters, Randolphs, Marshals and Calhouns.
And could a land that boasts a mind like this —
That bord'ring on the clime of freedom is —
Suffer a harlot with her whorings vile
To peacefully pollute her gen'rous soil?
Yes, green Kentucky with her native pride,
Proclaiming trust in the great Crucified,
Flaunting her prestige in the world's wide face,
Boasting descent and precedence of race,
And by the greatest of all statesmen led,
Shared the pollutions of a slavish bed.
All o'er her fields, the blood-hound's savage bay
Pressed the poor sable trembling runaway,
And sometimes by the home of Henry Clay!

*   *   *

I love Kentucky; tho' she merit scorn
I can't despise the land where I was born.
Her name I cherish, and expect to see
The day when all her sons will cherish me.
Her many sins have all in common been
With other sisters' who their sins have seen.
Yes, I will pray for that good time to come
When I can say: Kentucky is my *home*.
And this I now ask at my country's hand,
If I must die in some far distant land,
Then let my countrymen, when I am dead,
Where I was born, make my eternal bed.

*   *   *

Hail dawning Peace! Speed on thy glorious rise!
And with thy beams unseal the nation's eyes.
Let Islam in the blaze of scimitar
Proclaim his rites, and gorge the fangs of war,
But peace be unto thee, land of our sires,
Whose sacred altar flames with holier fires!
Let lawlessness no longer stagger forth
With his destructive torch, nor South nor North;
And let the humblest tenant of the fields,
Secured of what his honest labor yields,
Pursue his calling, ply his daily care,
His home adorn and helpless children rear,
Assured that while our flag above him flies,
No lawless hand can dare molest his joys.

*   *   *

Free schools, free press, free speech and equal laws,
A common country and a common cause,
Are only worthy of a freeman's boasts —
Are Freedom's *real* and intrinsic costs.
Without these, Freedom is an empty name,
And war-worn glory is a glaring shame.
Soon where yon happy future now appears,
Where learning now her glorious temple rears,
Our country's hosts shall round one interest meet,
And her free heart with one proud impulse beat,
One common blood thro' her life's channels flow,
While one great speech her loyal tongue shall know.
And soon, whoever to our bourne shall come,
Jew, Greek or Goth, he here shall be at home.
Then Ign'rance shall forsake her crooked ways,
And poor old Caste there end her feeble days.

FROM TWASINTA'S SEMINOLES; OR RAPE OF FLORIDA

Canto I.

INVOCATION.

I.

The poet hath a realm within, and throne,
And in his own soul singeth his lament.
A comer often in the world unknown —
A flaming minister to mortals sent;
In an apocalypse of sentiment
He shows in colors true the right or wrong,
And lights the soul of virtue with content;
Oh! could the world without him please us long?
What truth is there that lives and does not live in song?

II.

"The stuff's in him of robust manliness,
He is a poet, singing more by ear
Than note." His great heart filled with tenderness,
Thus spoke the patriarch bard of Cedarmere
Of me, who dwelt in a most obscure sphere;
For I was in the tents of bondage when
The muse inspired, and ere my song grew clear,
The graceful Bryant called his fellow-men
To mark what in my lay seemed pleasing to him then.

*   *   *

XIX.

Oh! sing it in the light of freedom's morn,
Tho' tyrant wars have made the earth a grave;
The good, the great, and true, are, if so, born,
And so with slaves, *chains do not make the slave!*
If high-souled birth be what the mother gave, —
If manly birth, and manly to the core, —
Whate'er the test, the man will he behave!
Crush him to earth and crush him o'er and o'er,
A man he'll rise at last and meet you as before.

XX.

So with our young Atlassa, hero-born, —
Free as the air within his palmy shade,
The nobler traits that do the man adorn,

In him were native: Not the music made
In Tampa's forests or the everglade
Was fitter, than in this young Seminole
Was the proud spirit which did life pervade,
And glow and tremble in his ardent soul —
Which, lit his inmost-self, and spurned all mean control.

*   *   *

XXXIII.

"Come now, my love, the moon is on the lake;
Upon the waters is my light canoe;
Come with me, love, and gladsome oars shall make
A music on the parting wave for you, —
Come o'er the waters deep and dark and blue;
Come where the lilies in the marge have sprung,
Come with me, love, for Oh, my love is true!"
This is the song that on the lake was sung,
The boatman sang it over when his heart was young.

XXXIV.

The boatman's song is hushed; the night is still,
Still as the vault of heaven, — a plashy oar
Starts from the shadows by the darkling hill,
And softly dips towards the farther shore;
Now stops, now dips again — is heard no more.
But follow the nook by yonder tree, —
Where spouts a tiny stream with fretish roar,
His light canoe is riding noiselessly —
A Chieftain's light canoe, in which his maid you see.

*   *   *

Canto II.

VII.

'T is hard to judge if hatred of one's race,
By those who deem themselves superior-born,
Be worse than that quiesence in disgrace,
Which only merits — and *should* only — scorn!
Oh! let me see the negro, night and morn,
Pressing and fighting in, for place and power!
If he a proud escutcheon would adorn,

All earth is place — all time th' auspicious hour,
While heaven leans forth to see, oh! can he quail or cower?

VIII.

Ah! I abhor his protest and complaint!
His pious looks and patience I despise!
He can't evade the test, disguised as saint,
The manly voice of freedom bids him rise,
And shake himself before Philistine eyes!
And, like a lion roused, no sooner than
A foe dare come, play all his energies,
And court the fray with fury if he can;
For hell itself respects a fearless manly man!

☆   ☆   ☆

XI.

I never was a slave — a robber took
My substance — what of that? The *law* my rights —
And that? I still was free and had my book —
All nature. And I learned from during hights
How silence is majestic, and invites
In admiration far beholding eyes!
And heaven taught me, with her starry nights,
How deepest speech unuttered often lies,
And that Jehovah's lessons mostly he implies.

HENRIETTA CORDELIA RAY (1850?–1916)

A New York City schoolteacher for 30 years, Ray published two collections of 146 poems whose technique is unusually rich.

ROBERT G. SHAW[*]

When War's red banners trailed along the sky,
And many a manly heart grew all aflame
With patriotic love and purest aim,
There rose a noble soul who dared to die,
If only Right could win. He heard the cry

---

[*] Shaw (1837–1863), a white army officer, was killed leading the all-black 54th Massachusetts Regiment in battle.

Of struggling bondmen and he quickly came,
Leaving the haunts where Learning tenders fame
Unto her honored sons; for it was ay
A loftier cause that lured him on to death.
Brave men who saw their brothers held in chains,
Beneath his standard battled ardently.
O friend! O hero! thou who yielded breath
That others might share Freedom's priceless gains,
In rev'rent love we guard thy memory.

VERSES TO MY HEART'S-SISTER

We've traveled long together,
        O sister of my heart,
Since first as little children
        All buoyant, we did start
Upon Life's checkered pathway,
        Nor dreamed of aught save joy;
But ah! To-day can tell us
        Naught is without alloy.

Rememb'rest thou the gambols
        Of those sweet, early days,
When siren Fancy showed us
        Our dreams through golden haze?
Ah, well thou dost remember
        The mirth we then did share,
The sports, the tasks, the music,
        The all-embracing prayer.

Somehow my own sweet sister,
        Our heart-strings early twined;
Some rare bond of affection
        Of tastes and aims combined;
Made us, e'en in our Springtime,
        Soul-sisters fond and leal;
And how that love has strengthened
        The years can well reveal.

We've seen our loved ones vanish
        Far from our yearning gaze,
Into the peace of Heaven.
        O those sad, saddest days,
When we two clung together,
        So lonely and forlorn,

With our crushed hearts all quiv'ring,
 All bruised, and scarred and torn.

So nearer clung we, sister,
 And loved each other more;
The tendrils of our natures
 Twined closer than before.
We could speak to no other
 Of those sweet, holy things,
So tender yet so nameless,
 Which sorrow often brings.

The troubles that have thickened
 Around our daily path,
We've borne together, sister,
 And oft when courage hath
Grown feeble, and the future
 Was dark with naught of cheer,
Could one have faced the conflict
 Without the other near?

And sister, dear Heart's-Sister,
 When all the mystery
Of this strange life is ended
 In Immortality,
We'll love each other dearly
 As now we do, and more;
For sacred things in Heaven
 Grow richer than before.

And shall not those sweet loved ones
 Missed here so long! so long!
Join with us in the music
 Of an all-perfect song?
We feel a gladder cadence
 Will thrill their rapt'rous strain,
When we are with them, sister,
 All, ne'er to part again!

So now as here we linger,
 May ours be happy days!
O generous-hearted sister,
 In all Life's winding ways
May we have joy together!
 And this I fondly pray, —
God bless thee, dear Heart's-Sister!
 Forever and for aye!

GEORGE MARION McCLELLAN (1860–1934)

A minister, teacher, fiction writer and poet from Tennessee, McClellan was highly educated and a man of deep faith, personal courage and sensitivity to his role as a black man in white society.

A SEPTEMBER NIGHT

The full September moon sheds floods of light,
And all the bayou's face is gemmed with stars
Save where are dropped fantastic shadows down
From sycamores and moss-hung cypress trees.
With slumberous sound the waters half asleep
Creep on and on their way, twixt rankish reeds,
Through marsh and lowlands stretching to the gulf.
Begirt with cotton fields Anguilla sits
Half bird-like dreaming on her summer nest
Amid her spreading figs, and roses still
In bloom with all their spring and summer hues.
Pomegranates hang with dapple cheeks full ripe,
And over all the town a dreamy haze
Drops down. The great plantations stretching far
Away are plains of cotton downy white.
O, glorious is this night of joyous sounds
Too full for sleep. Aromas wild and sweet,
From muscadine, late blooming jessamine,
And roses, all the heavy air suffuse.
Faint bellows from the alligators come
From swamps afar, where sluggish lagoons give
To them a peaceful home. The katydids
Make ceaseless cries. Ten thousand insects' wings
Stir in the moonlight haze and joyous shouts
Of Negro song and mirth awake hard by
The cabin dance. O, glorious is this night.
The summer sweetness fills my heart with songs
I cannot sing, with loves I cannot speak.

THE FEET OF JUDAS

Christ washed the feet of Judas!
The dark and evil passions of his soul,
His secret plot, and sordidness complete,

His hate, his purposing, Christ knew the whole,
And still in love he stooped and washed his feet.

Christ washed the feet of Judas!
Yet all his lurking sin was bare to him,
His bargain with the priest and more than this,
In Olivet beneath the moonlight dim,
Aforehand knew and felt his treacherous kiss.

Christ washed the feet of Judas!
And so ineffable his love 'twas meet,
That pity fill his great forgiving heart,
And tenderly to wash the traitor's feet,
Who in his Lord had basely sold his part.

Christ washed the feet of Judas!
And thus a girded servant, self-abased,
Taught that no wrong this side the gate of heaven
Was e'er too great to wholly be effaced,
And though unasked, in spirit be forgiven.

And so if we have ever felt the wrong
Of trampled rights, of caste, it matters not,
Whate'er the soul has felt or suffered long,
Oh heart! this one thing should not be forgot,
Christ washed the feet of Judas!

A JANUARY DANDELION

All Nashville is a chill. And everywhere
Like desert sand, when the winds blow,
There is each moment sifted through the air,
A powdered blast of January snow.
O! thoughtless Dandelion, to be misled
By a few warm days to leave thy natural bed,
Was folly growth and blooming over soon.
And yet, thou blasted yellow-coated gem,
Full many a heart has but a common boon
With thee, now freezing on thy slender stem.
When the heart has bloomed by the touch of love's warm breath
Then left and chilling snow is sifted in,
It still may beat but there is blast and death
To all that blooming life that might have been.

JOSEPH SEAMON COTTER, SR. (1861–1949)

A prominent educator and worker for racial progress, Cotter published nine books of poetry, plays and fiction on wide-ranging historical, philosophical and social themes.

FREDERICK DOUGLASS

O eloquent and caustic sage!
Thy long and rugged pilgrimage
    To glory's shrine has ended;
And thou hast passed the inner door,
And proved thy fitness o'er and o'er,
    And to the dome ascended.

In speaking of thy noble life
One needs must think upon the strife
    That long and sternly faced it;
But since those times have flitted by,
Just let the useless relic die
    With passions that embraced it.

There is no evil known to man
But what, if wise enough, he can
    Grow stronger in the bearing;
And so the ills we often scorn
May be of heavenly wisdom born
    To aid our onward faring.

Howe'er this be, just fame has set
Her jewels in thy coronet
    So firmly that the ages
To come will ever honor thee
And place thy name in company
    With patriots and sages.

Now thou art gone, the little men
Of fluent tongue and trashy pen
    Will strive to imitate thee;
And when they find they haven't sense
Enough to make a fair pretense,
    They'll turn and underrate thee.

DR. BOOKER T. WASHINGTON TO THE NATIONAL NEGRO BUSINESS LEAGUE

'Tis strange indeed to hear us plead
    For selling and for buying
When yesterday we said: "Away
    With all good things but dying."

The world's ago, and we're agog
    To have our first brief inning;
So let's away through surge and fog
    However slight the winning.

What deeds have sprung from plow and pick!
    What bank-rolls from tomatoes!
No dainty crop of rhetoric
    Can match one of potatoes.

Ye orators of point and pith,
    Who force the world to heed you,
What skeletons you'll journey with
    Ere it is forced to feed you.

A little gold won't mar our grace,
    A little ease our glory.
This world's a better biding place
    When money clinks its story.

THE DON'T-CARE NEGRO

Neber min' what's in your cran'um
    So your collar's high an' true.
Neber min' what's in your pocket
    So de blackin's on your shoe.

Neber min' who keeps you comp'ny
    So he halfs up what he's tuk.
Neber min' what way you's gwine
    So you's gwine away frum wuk.

Neber min' de race's troubles
    So you profits by dem all.
Neber min' your leaders' stumblin'
    So you he'ps to mak' dem fall.

Neber min' what's true tomorrow
    So you libes a dream today.

Neber min' what tax is levied
    So it's not on craps or play.

Neber min' how hard you labors
    So you does it to de en'
Dat de judge is boun' to sen' you
    An' your record to de "pen."

Neber min' your manhood's risin'
    So you habe a way to stay it.
Neber min' folks' good opinion
    So you habe a way to slay it.

Neber min' man's why an' wharfo'
    So de world is big an' roun'.
Neber min' whar next you's gwine to
    So you's six foot under groun'.

JOSEPHINE DELPHINE HENDERSON HEARD
(1861–1921)

The daughter of North Carolina slaves, Heard received a good education, taught school and married A. M. E. Bishop William Henry Heard, with whom she traveled throughout the world.

"THEY ARE COMING?"

They are coming, coming slowly —
They are coming, surely, surely —
In each avenue you hear the steady tread.
From the depths of foul oppression,
Comes a swarthy-hued procession,
And victory perches on their banners' head.

They are coming, coming slowly —
They are coming; yes, the lowly,
No longer writhing in their servile bands.
From the rice fields and plantation
Comes a factor of the nation,
And threatening, like Banquo's ghost, it stands.

They are coming, coming proudly —
They are crying, crying loudly:
O, for justice from the rulers of the land!

And that justice will be given,
For the mighty God of heaven
Holds the balances of power in his hand.

Prayers have risen, risen, risen,
From the cotton fields and prison;
Though the overseer stood with lash in hand,
Groaned the overburdened heart;
Not a tear-drop dared to start —
But the Slaves' petition reach'd the glory-land.

They are coming, they are coming,
From away in tangled swamp,
Where the slimy reptile hid its poisonous head;
Through the long night and the day,
They have heard the bloodhounds' bey,
While the morass furnished them an humble bed.

They are coming, rising, rising,
And their progress is surprising,
By their brawny muscles earning daily bread;
Though their wages be a pittance,
Still each week a small remittance,
Builds a shelter for the weary toiling head.

They are coming, they are coming —
Listen! You will hear the humming
Of the thousands that are falling into line:
There are Doctors, Lawyers, Preachers;
There are Sculptors, Poets, Teachers —
Men and women, who with honor yet shall shine.

They are coming, coming boldly,
Though the Nation greets them coldly;
They are coming from the hillside and the plain.
With their scars they tell the story
Of the canebrakes wet and gory,
Where their brothers' bones lie bleaching with the slain.

They are coming, coming singing,
Their Thanksgiving hymn is ringing.
For the clouds are slowly breaking now away,
And there comes a brighter dawning —
It is liberty's fair morning,
They are coming surely, coming, clear the way.

Yes, they come, their stepping's steady,
And their power is felt already —

God has heard the lowly cry of the oppressed:
And beneath his mighty frown,
Every wrong shall crumble down,
When the *right* shall triumph and the world be blest!

DANIEL WEBSTER DAVIS (1862–1913)

Davis was an educator, Baptist minister, popular orator, historian, poet and a leader of Richmond, Virginia's African-American community for over three decades.

I CAN TRUST

I can not see why trials come,
And sorrows follow thick and fast;
I can not fathom His designs,
Nor why my pleasures can not last,
Nor why my hopes so soon are dust,
But, I can trust.

When darkest clouds my sky o'er hang,
And sadness seems to fill the land,
I calmly trust His promise sweet,
And cling to his ne'er failing hand,
And, in life's darkest hour, I'll just
Look up and trust.

I know my life with Him is safe,
And all things still must work for good
To those who love and serve our God,
And lean on Him as children should,
Though hopes decay and turn to dust,
I still will trust.

AUNT CHLOE'S LULLABY

Hesh! my baby; stop yer fuss,
I's 'fraid yuz gittin wuss an' wuss;
Doncher cry, an' I gwy mek'
Mammy's baby 'lasses cake.
Hesh! my lubly baby chil',
I gwy rock yo' all de whil';

Nuffin gwyne to ketch yo' now,
'Cause yer mammy's watchin' yo'.
Sleep! my little baby, sleep!
    Mammy's baby, Lou!

How dem dogs do bark to-night!
Better shet yer eyes up tight;
Dey kan't hab dis baby dear;
Mammy's watchin', doncher fear.
Hear dem owls a-hootin' so?
Dey shan't ketch dis baby, do'.
Jes' like mistis lub her chil',
Mammy lubs dis baby too.
Sleep! my little baby, sleep!
    Mammy's baby, Lou!

Mammy's baby, black an' sweet,
Jes' like candy dat you eat,
Mammy lay yo' in dis bed,
While she mek de whi' folk's bread.
Angels dey gwy look below,
Watch dis baby sleepin' so.
Go to sleep, my hunny, now,
Ain't yer mammy watchin' yo'?
Sleep! my little baby, sleep!
    Mammy's baby, Lou.

MARY WESTON FORDHAM (1862?–?)

In subject and tone, Fordham's poetry resembles the work of white "female poets" of the nineteenth century, sentimentalizing death, motherhood, nature and Christian faith.

ATLANTA EXPOSITION ODE

"Cast down your bucket where you are,"
From burning sands or Polar star
From where the iceberg rears its head
Or where the kingly palms outspread;
'Mid blackened fields or golden sheaves,
Or foliage green, or autumn leaves,
Come sounds of warning from afar,
"Cast down your bucket where you are."

What doth it matter if thy years
Have slowly dragged 'mid sighs and tears?
What doth it matter, since thy day
Is brightened now by hope's bright ray.
The morning star will surely rise,
And Ethiop's sons with longing eyes
And outstretched hands, will bless the day,
When old things shall have passed away.

Come, comrades, from the East, the West!
Come, bridge the chasm. It is best.
Come, warm hearts of the sunny South,
And clasp hands with the mighty North.
Rise Afric's sons and chant with joy,
Good will to all without alloy;
The night of grief has passed away —
On Orient gleams a brighter day.

Say, ye that wore the blue, how sweet
That thus in sympathy we meet,
Our brothers who the gray did love
And martyrs to their cause did prove.
Say, once for all and once again,
That blood no more shall flow in vain;
Say Peace shall brood o'er this fair land
And hearts, for aye, be joined with hand.

Hail! Watchman, from thy lofty height;
Tell us, O tell us of the night?
Will Bethlehem's Star ere long arise
And point this nation to the skies?
Will pæans ring from land and sea
Fraught with untrammelled liberty
Till Time's appointed course be run,
And Earth's millenium be begun?

"Cast down your bucket," let it be
As water flows both full and free!
Let charity, that twice blest boon
Thy watchword be from night to morn.
Let kindness as the dew distil
To friend and foe, alike, good will;
Till sounds the wondrous battle-call,
For all one flag, one flag for all.

JAMES EDWIN CAMPBELL (1867–1896)

An educator and journalist, Campbell created dynamic folk verses in "Gullah" dialect that were universally praised for their originality, hard realism, authentic voice and spirit and apt musicality.

OL' DOC' HYAR

Ur ol' Hyar lib in ur house on de hill,
He hunner yurs ol' an' nebber wuz ill;
He yurs dee so long an' he eyes so beeg,
An' he laigs so spry dat he dawnce ur jeeg;
He lib so long dat he know ebbry tings
'Bout de beas'ses dat walks an' de bu'ds dat sings —
        Dis Ol' Doc' Hyar,
        Whar lib up dar
Een ur mighty fine house on ur mighty high hill.

He doctah fur all de beas'ses an' bu'ds —
He put on he specs an' he use beeg wu'ds,
He feel dee pu's' den he look mighty wise,
He pull out he watch an' he shet bofe eyes;
He grab up he hat an' grab up he cane,
Den — "blam!" go de do' — he gone lak de train,
        Dis Ol' Doc' Hyar,
        Whar lib up dar
Een ur mighty fine house on ur mighty high hill.

Mistah Ba'r fall sick — dee sont fur Doc' Hyar,
"O, Doctah, come queeck, an' see Mr. B'ar;
He mighty nigh daid des sho' ez you b'on!"
"Too much ur young peeg, too much ur green co'n,"
Ez he put on he hat, said Ol' Doc' Hyar;
"I'll tek 'long meh lawnce, an' lawnce Mistah B'ar,"
        Said Ol' Doc' Hyar,
        Whar lib up dar
Een ur mighty fine house on ur mighty high hill.

Mistah B'ar he groaned, Mistah B'ar he growled,
W'ile de ol' Mis' B'ar an' de chillen howled;
Doctah Hyar tuk out he sha'p li'l lawnce,
An' pyu'ced Mistah B'ar twel he med him prawnce
Den grab up he hat an' grab up he cane
"Blam!" go de do' an' he gone lak de train,

        Dis Ol' Doc' Hyar,
        Whar lib up dar
Een ur mighty fine house on ur mighty high hill.

But de vay naix day Mistah B'ar he daid;
Wen dee tell Doc' Hyar, he des scratch he haid:
"Ef pashons git well ur pashons git wu's,
Money got ter come een de Ol' Hyar's pu's;
Not wut folkses does, but fur wut dee know
Does de folkses git paid" — an' Hyar larfed low,
        Dis sma't Ol' Hyar,
        Whar lib up dar
Een de mighty fine house on de mighty high hill!

MORS ET VITA[*]

Into the soil a seed is sown,
Out of the soul a song is wrung,
Out of the shell a pearl is gone,
Out of the cage a bird is flown,
    Out of the body, a soul!

Unto a tree the seed is grown,
Wide in the world the song is sung,
The pearl in a necklace gleams more fair,
The bird is flown to a sweeter air,
And Death is half and Life is half,
    And the two make up the whole!

DE CUNJAH MAN

O chillen run, de Cunjah man,
Him mouf ez beeg ez fryin' pan,
Him yurs am small, him eyes am raid,
Him hab no toof een him ol' haid,
Him hab him roots, him wu'k him trick,
Him roll him eye, him mek you sick —
   De Cunjah man, de Cunjah man,
   O chillen run, de Cunjah man!

Him hab ur ball ob raid, raid ha'r,
Him hide it un' de kitchen sta'r,
Mam Jude huh pars urlong dat way,

---

[*] [Death and Life]

An' now huh hab ur snaik, dey say.
Him wrop ur roun' huh buddy tight,
Huh eyes pop out, ur orful sight —
    De Cunjah man, de Cunjah man,
    O chillen run, de Cunjah man!

Miss Jane, huh dribe him f'um huh do',
An' now huh hens woan' lay no mo';
De Jussey cow huh done fall sick,
Hit all done by de cunjah trick.
Him put ur root un' 'Lijah's baid,
An' now de man he sho' am daid —
    De Cunjah man, de Cunjah man,
    O chillen run, de Cunjah man!

Me see him stan' de yudder night
Right een de road een white moon-light;
Him toss him arms, him whirl him 'roun',
Him stomp him foot urpon de groun';
De snaiks come crawlin', one by one,
Me hyuh um hiss, me break an' run —
    De Cunjah man, de Cunjah man,
    O chillen run, de Cunjah man!

'SCIPLININ' SISTER BROWN

Shet up dat noise, you chillen! Dar's some one at de do'.
Dribe out dem dogs; you 'Rastus, tek Linkum off de flo'!

Des ma'ch yo'se'f right in sah! (Jane, tek dem ashes out!
Dis house look lak ur hog-pen; you M'randy, jump erbout!)

W'y bress my soul, hit's Ef'um — w'y, Ef'um, how you do?
An' Tempie an' de chillen? I hopes dey's all well too.

Hyuh, M'randy, bresh dat stool off; now, Ef'um, des set down.
Wut's de news f'um off de Ridge an' wut's de news in town?

Now doan' you t'ink dem niggahs hed Susan 'fo de chu'ch
'Bout dawncin' at de pa'ty — dey call dat sinnin' much.

Dey up an' call ur meetin' ter 'scipline Sistah Brown,
But de night dey hol' de meetin' she tuk herse'f to town.

Dey sont de Bo'd ob Deacons, de pahstah at de head,
Ter wait urpon de sistah an' pray wid her, dey said,

But Susan mighty stubbo'n, an' wen dey lif' ur pra'r
She up an' tell de deacons she des wawn' gwine ter cyar.

An' wen de Reb'ren' Pa'son prayed 'bout ur "sheep wuz los'."
An' 'bout de "po bac'slidah," she gin her head ur toss!

I seed de debbil raisin' in de white ob Susan's eyes —
Fyeah she blow dat deacon-bo'd ter "mansions in de skies,"

I des tuk down my bawnjer an' den I 'gins an' plays;
"Come dy fount ob ebbry blessin', chune my ha't ter sing dy praise."

De pa'son an' de deacons dey jined me pooty soon;
Lawd! Dat bawnjer shuk itse'f ur-playin' ob de chune!

An' wen dey mos' wuz shoutin', I tightened up er string,
Drapped right inter "Money Musk" an' gin de chune full swing.

De "Debbil's Dream" come arter — de debbil wuz ter pay,
Dem niggahs fell ter pattin' — I larf mos' ebbry day!

Deacon Jones got on his feet, de pa'son pulled him down;
I played ur little fastah, an' sho's my name am Brown,

De pa'son an' de deacons jined han's right on dis flo',
Su'cled right and su'cled lef' — it sutny wuz ur show.

Dey 'naded up an' down de flo' an' w'en hit come ter swing,
De pa'son gin hisse'f a flirt an' cut de pidgin-wing!

An' we'n urfo' de meetin' dat 'mittee med its 'po't
'Bout Sistah Susan's dawncin', dey cut it mighty sho't.

De chyuhsman, Mr. Pa'son, said in tones so mil' an' sweet:
"Sistah Brown wa'n't guilty, caze — SHE NEBBER CROSSED HER FEET!"

JAMES DAVID CORROTHERS (1869–1919)

A newspaperman and minister, Corrothers published poems and essays in national periodicals and in three collections, plus a well-received auto-biography.

"DE BLACK CAT CROSSED HIS LUCK"

I

"O, de Black Cat cotch ole Sambo Lee,
As he come home f'om a jamboree!
De cat sot up in a juniper tree,
Shakin' ob his sides wid glee.
De moon was sailin' oberhead —
Sam's h'aht felt lak a lump o' lead.
Black Cat grinned an' wonk one eye,
Licked his paws an' gib a sigh,
An' den he cried: 'Me-ow, me-ow —
Upon ma soul ah'm got you now!
Fall down an' pray, po' cullud man,
Foh de ole Black Cat done call yo' han'.'

II

"Sam los' his job de very nex' day;
An' when he went to git his pay,
Got bit by a po' man's dog —
Policeman beat him wid his log —
Got arrested, put in jail —
Had to hustle hahd foh bail —
Lost his lawsuit, sprained his jaw
Wranglin' wid his mother-in-law —
Lost his best ob lady lubs —
Got knocked out wid de boxin' glubs —
Got hel' up an' lost his roll —
Robber almose took his soul!
Sam went to de hospital —
Three weeks passed 'fo' he got well.
Played de races — got broke flat;
An' all because ob dat Black Cat!

III

"Den to de cunjah-man Sam sped,
An' dis am whut de cunjah-man said:
'Black Cat am a pow'ful man;
Ruinin' mo'tals am his plan.
Ole Satan an' de 'Riginal Sin
Am de daddy an' mammy o' him.
He's got nine hunderd an' ninety-nine libes —
Nineteen thousan' an' ninety-nine wibes —
He's kin to cholera an' allied
To smallpox on de mammy's side.
An' all de ebils on de earf
Stahted at de Black Cat's birf! —
Jes' stop an' die right whah you's at,
Ef yo' luck bin crossed by de ole Black Cat!'

IV

"An' den Sam read in history
Dat a cat crossed Pharaoh by de see,
An' burried him, as sho's you bo'n,
Too deep to heah ole Gabriel's ho'n!
An' dat de cat crossed Jonah once,
An' made him ack a regular dunce.
Crossed Bonaparte at Waterloo,
An' got Jeems Blaine defeated, too.
'Oh, Laud a-mussy now on me!'
Cried Sam, 'an' on dis history!'
An' den Sam went an' killed de cat —
Swo'e he'd make an end o' dat; —
Burried him in de light o' de moon,
Wid a rabbit's foot an' a silver spoon.
But de Black Cat riz, an' swallered him whole —
Bu'nt his house an' took his soul!"

PAUL LAURENCE DUNBAR

He came, a youth, singing in the dawn
    Of a new freedom, glowing o'er his lyre,
    Refining, as with great Apollo's fire,
    His people's gift of song. And thereupon,
This Negro singer, come to Helicon,
Constrained the masters, listening to admire,
And roused a race to wonder and aspire,

Gazing which way their honest voice was gone,
With ebon face uplit of glory's crest.
   Men marveled at the singer, strong and sweet,
   Who brought the cabin's mirth, the tuneful night,
But faced the morning, beautiful with light,
   To die while shadows yet fell toward the west,
   And leave his laurels at his people's feet.

Dunbar, no poet wears your laurels now;
   None rises, singing, from your race like you.
   Dark melodist, immortal, though the dew
   Fell early on the bays upon your brow,
And tinged with pathos every halcyon vow
   And brave endeavor. Silence o'er you threw
   Flowerets of love. Or, if an envious few
Of your own people brought no garlands, how
Could malice smite him whom the gods had crowned?
   If, like the meadow-lark, your flight was low,
   Your flooded lyrics half the hilltops drowned;
A wide world heard you, and it loved you so,
   It stilled its heart to list the strains you sang,
   And o'er your happy songs its plaudits rang.

AT THE CLOSED GATE OF JUSTICE

To be a Negro in a day like this
   Demands forgiveness. Bruised with blow on blow,
Betrayed, like him whose woe dimmed eyes gave bliss,
   Still must one succor those who brought one low,
To be a Negro in a day like this.

To be a Negro in a day like this
   Demands rare patience — patience that can wait
In utter darkness. 'Tis the path to miss,
   And knock, unheeded, at an iron gate,
To be a Negro in a day like this.

To be a Negro in a day like this
   Demands strange loyalty. We serve a flag
Which is to us white freedom's emphasis.
   Ah! one must love when Truth and Justice lag,
To be a Negro in a day like this.

To be a Negro in a day like this —
   Alas! Lord God, what evil have we done?

Still shines the gate, all gold and amethyst,
  But I pass by, the glorious goal unwon,
"Merely a Negro" — in a day like this!

AN INDIGNATION DINNER

Dey was hard times jes fo' Christmas round our neighborhood one year;
So we held a secret meetin', whah de white folks couldn't hear,
To 'scuss de situation, an' to see what could be done
Towa'd a fust-class Christmas dinneh an' a little Christmas fun.

Rufus Green, who called de meetin', ris an' said: "In dis here town,
An' throughout de land, de white folks is a'tryin' to keep us down."
S' 'e: "Dey bought us, sold us, beat us; now dey 'buse us 'ca'se we's free;
But when dey tetch my stomach, dey's done gone too fur foh me!

"Is I right?" "You sho is, Rufus!" roared a dozen hungry throats.
"Ef you'd keep a mule a-wo'kin', don't you tamper wid his oats.
Dat's sense," continued Rufus. "But dese white folks nowadays
Has done got so close and stingy you can't live on what dey pays.

"Here 'tis Christmas-time, an', folkses, I's indignant 'nough to choke.
Whah's our Christmas dinneh comin' when we's 'mos' completely broke?
I can't hahdly 'fo'd a toothpick an' a glass o' water. Mad?
Say, I'm desp'ret! Dey jes better treat me nice, dese white folks had!"

Well, dey 'bused de white folks scan'lous, till old Pappy Simmons ris,
Leanin' on his cane to s'pote him, on account his rheumatis',
An' s' 'e: "Chilun, whut's dat wintry wind a-sighin' th'ough de street
'Bout yo' wasted summeh wages? But, no matter, we mus' eat.

"Now, I seed a beau'ful tuhkey on a certain gemmun's fahm.
He's a-growin' fat an' sassy, an' a-struttin' to a chahm.
Chickens, sheeps, hogs, sweet pertaters — all de craps is fine dis year;
All we needs is a committee foh to tote de goodies here."

Well, we lit right in an' voted dat it was a gran' idee,
An' de dinneh we had Christmas was worth trabblin' miles to see;
An' we eat a full an' plenty, big an' little, great an' small,
Not beca'se we was dishonest, but indignant, sah. Dat's all.

JAMES WELDON JOHNSON (1871–1938)

An educator, lawyer, newspaperman, United States consular officer and secretary of the NAACP, Johnson was a versatile man of letters: a librettist and songwriter, novelist, historian, anthologist, autobiographer and poet.

LIFT EV'RY VOICE AND SING

(the "Negro National Anthem")
Music by J. Rosamond Johnson

Lift every voice and sing
Till earth and heaven ring,
Ring with the harmonies of Liberty;
Let our rejoicing rise
High as the listening skies
Let it resound loud as the rolling sea.
Sing a song full of the faith that the dark past has taught us,
Sing a song full of the hope that the present has brought us.
Facing the rising sun of our new day begun,
Let us march on till victory is won.

Stony the road we trod,
Bitter the chastening rod,
Felt in the days when hope unborn died;
Yet with a steady beat,
Have not our weary feet
Come to the place for which our fathers sighed?
We have come over a way that with tears has been watered.
We have come, treading our path through the blood of the slaugh-
    tered.
Out from the gloomy past,
Till now we stand at last
Where the white gleam of our bright star is cast.

God of our weary years,
God of our silent tears,
Thou who has brought us thus far on the way;
Thou who hast by Thy might
Led us into the light,
Keep us forever in the path, we pray.
Lest our feet stray from the places, our God, where we meet Thee;
Lest our hearts drunk with the vine of the world we forget thee,

Shadowed beneath Thy hand,
May we forever stand,
True to our God,
True to our native land.

O BLACK AND UNKNOWN BARDS

O black and unknown bards of long ago,
How came your lips to touch the sacred fire?
How, in your darkness, did you come to know
The power and beauty of the minstrel's lyre?
Who first from midst his bonds lifted his eyes?
Who first from out the still watch, lone and long,
Feeling the ancient faith of prophets rise
Within his dark-kept soul, burst into song?

Heart of what slave poured out such melody
As "Steal away to Jesus"? On its strains
His spirit must have nightly floated free,
Though still about his hands he felt his chains.
Who heard great "Jordan roll"? Whose starward eye
Saw chariot "swing low"? And who was he
That breathed that comforting, melodic sigh,
"Nobody knows de trouble I see"?

What merely living clod, what captive thing,
Could up toward God through all its darkness grope,
And find within its deadened heart to sing
These songs of sorrow, love and faith, and hope?
How did it catch that subtle undertone,
That note in music heard not with the ears?
How sound the elusive reed so seldom blown,
Which stirs the soul or melts the heart to tears.

Not that great German master in his dream
Of harmonies that thundered amongst the stars
At the creation, ever heard a theme
Nobler than "Go down, Moses." Mark its bars
How like a mighty trumpet-call they stir
The blood. Such are the notes that men have sung
Going to valorous deeds; such tones there were
That helped make history when Time was young.

There is a wide, wide wonder in it all,
That from degraded rest and servile toil
The fiery spirit of the seer should call

These simple children of the sun and soil.
O black slave singers, gone, forgot, unfamed,
You — you alone, of all the long, long line
Of those who've sung untaught, unknown, unnamed,
Have stretched out upward, seeking the divine.

You sang not deeds of heroes or of kings;
No chant of bloody war, no exulting paean
Of arms-won triumphs; but your humble strings
You touched in chord with music empyrean.
You sang far better than you knew; the songs
That for your listeners' hungry hearts sufficed
Still live, — but more than this to you belongs:
You sang a race from wood and stone to Christ.

THE WHITE WITCH

O brothers mine, take care! Take care!
The great white witch rides out tonight.
Trust not your prowess nor your strength,
Your only safety lies in flight;
For in her glance there is a snare,
And in her smile there is a blight.

The great white witch you have not seen?
Then, younger brothers mine, forsooth,
Like nursery children you have looked
For ancient hag and snaggle-tooth;
But no, not so; the witch appears
In all the glowing charms of youth.

Her lips are like carnations, red,
Her face like new-born lilies, fair,
Her eyes like ocean waters, blue,
She moves with subtle grace and air,
And all about her head there floats
The golden glory of her hair.

But though she always thus appears
In form of youth and mood of mirth,
Unnumbered centuries are hers,
The infant planets saw her birth;
The child of throbbing Life is she,
Twin sister to the greedy earth.

And back behind those smiling lips,
And down within those laughing eyes,
And underneath the soft caress
Of hand and voice and purring sighs,
The shadow of the panther lurks,
The spirit of the vampire lies.

For I have seen the great white witch,
And she has led me to her lair,
And I have kissed her red, red lips
And cruel face so white and fair;
Around me she has twined her arms,
And bound me with her yellow hair.

I felt those red lips burn and sear
My body like a living coal;
Obeyed the power of those eyes
As the needle trembles to the pole;
And did not care although I felt
The strength go ebbing from my soul.

Oh! she has seen your strong young limbs,
And heard your laughter loud and gay,
And in your voices she has caught
The echo of a far-off day,
When man was closer to the earth;
And she has marked you for her prey.

She feels the old Antaean strength
In you, the great dynamic beat
Of primal passions, and she sees
In you the last besieged retreat
Of love relentless, lusty, fierce,
Love fain-ecstatic, cruel-sweet.

O brothers mine, take care! Take care!
The great white witch rides out tonight.
O younger brothers mine, beware!
Look not upon her beauty bright;
For in her glance there is a snare,
And in her smile there is a blight.

PRISCILLA JANE THOMPSON (1871–1942)

Christian faith, love and racial issues were Thompson's favorite topics.
She and her siblings, Clara Ann and Aaron Belford, privately published
seven volumes of verse between 1899 and 1926.

THE MUSE'S FAVOR

Oh Muse! I crave a favor,
  Grant but this one unto me;
Thou hast always been indulgent —
  So I boldly come to thee.

For oft I list thy singing —
  And the accents, sweet and clear,
Like the rhythmic flow of waters,
  Fall on my ecstatic ear.

But of Caucasia's daughters,
  So oft I've heard thy lay,
That the music, too familiar —
  Falls in sheer monotony.

And now, oh Muse exalted!
  Exchange this old song staid,
For an equally deserving —
  The oft slighted, Afric maids.

The Muse, with smiles consenting,
  Runs her hand the strings along,
And the harp, as bound by duty —
Rings out with the tardy song.

The Song

Oh, foully slighted Ethiope maid!
With patience, bearing rude upbraid,
With sweet, refined, retiring, grace,
And sunshine ling'ring in thy face,
With eyes bedewed and pityingly
  I sing of thee, I sing of thee.

Thy dark and misty curly hair,
In small, neat, braids entwineth fair,

Like clusters of rich, shining, jet,
All wrapt in mist, when sun is set;
Fair maid, I gaze admiringly,
   And sing of thee, and sing of thee.

Thy smooth and silky, dusky skin,
Thine eyes of sloe, thy dimple chin,
That pure and simple heart of thine,
   Tis these that make thee half divine;
Oh maid! I gaze admiringly,
And sing of thee, and sing of thee.

Oh modest maid, with beauty rare,
Whoe'er hath praised thy lithe form, fair?
Thy tender mein, thy fairy tread —
Thy winsome face and queenly head?
Naught of thy due in verse I see,
   All pityingly I sing of thee.

Who've dared to laud thee 'fore the world,
And face the stigma of a churl?
Or brook the fiery, deep, disdain —
Their portion, who defend thy name?
Oh maiden, wronged so cowardly.
   I boldly, loudly, sing of thee.

Who've stood the test of chastity,
Through slav'ry's blasting tyranny,
And kept the while, their virtuous grace,
   To instill in a trampled race?
   Fair maid, thy equal few may see;
   Thrice honored I, to sing of thee.

Let cowards fear thy name to praise,
Let scoffers seek thee but to raze;
Despite their foul, ignoble, jeers,
A worthy model thou appear,
Enrobed in love and purity;
   Oh who dare blush, to sing of thee?

And now, oh maid, forgive I pray,
The tardiness of my poor lay;
The weight of wrongs unto thee done —
Did paralize my falt'ring tongue;
'Twas my mute, innate, sympathy —
   That staid this song, I sing to thee.

PAUL LAURENCE DUNBAR (1872–1906)

Dunbar gained international renown and popularized black literature by lecturing and reading his poetry. He published prolifically: seven volumes of verse (over 400 poems); four novels; four collections of short stories; dozens of articles in magazines; song lyrics, musical plays and sketches.

SYMPATHY

I know what the caged bird feels, alas!
    When the sun is bright on the upland slopes;
When the wind stirs soft through the springing grass,
And the river flows like a stream of glass;
    When the first bird sings and the first bud opes,
And the faint perfume from its chalice steals —
I know what the caged bird feels!

I know why the caged bird beats his wing
    Till its blood is red on the cruel bars;
For he must fly back to his perch and cling
When he fain would be on the bough a-swing;
    And a pain still throbs in the old, old scars
And they pulse again with a keener sting —
I know why he beats his wing!

I know why the caged bird sings, ah me,
    When his wing is bruised and his bosom sore, —
When he beats his bars and he would be free;
It is not a carol of joy or glee,
    But a prayer that he sends from his heart's deep core,
But a plea, that upward to Heaven he flings —
I know why the caged bird sings!

AN ANTE-BELLUM SERMON

We is gathahed hyeah, my brothah,
    In dis howlin' wildaness,
Fer to speak some words of comfo't
    To each othah in distress.
An' we chooses fer ouah subjic'
    Dis — we'll 'splain it by an' by;
"An' de Lawd said Moses, Moses,
    An' de man said, 'Hyeah am I.' "

Now ole Pher'oh, down in Egypt,
    Was de wuss man evah bo'n,
An' he had de Hebrew chillun,
    Down dah wukin' in his co'n;
'Twell de Lawd got tiahed o' his foolin;
    An' sez he: "I'll let him know —
Look hyeah, Moses, go tell Pher'oh
    Fu' to let dem chillen go.

An' ef he refuse to do it,
    I will make him rue de houah,
Fu' I'll empty down on Egypt
    All de vials of my powah."
Yes, he did — an' Pher'oh's ahmy
    Wasn't wuth a ha'f a dime;
Fu' de Lawd will he'p his chillun,
    You kin trust him ev'ry time.

An' yo' enemies may 'sail you
    In de back an' in de front;
But de Lawd is all aroun' you,
    Fu' to ba' de battle's brunt.
Dey kin fo'ge yo' chains an' shackles
    F'om de mountains to de sea;
But de Lawd will sen' some Moses
    Fu' to set his chillun free.

An' de lan' shall hyeah his thundah,
    Lak a blas' f'om Gab'el's ho'n,
Fu' de Lawd of hosts is mighty
    When he girds his ahmor on.
But fu' feah some one mistakes me,
    I will pause right hyeah to say,
Dat I'm still a-preachin' ancient,
    I ain't talkin' 'bout to-day.

But I tell you, fellah christuns,
    Things'll happen mighty strange;
Now, de Lawd done dis fu' Isrul,
    An' his ways don't nevah change,
An' de love he showed to Isrul
    Wasn't all on Isrul spent;
Now don't run an' tell yo' mastahs
    Dat I'se preachin' discontent.

'Cause I isn't; I'se a judgin'
　　Bible people by deir ac's;
I'se a givin' you de Scriptuah,
　　I'se a handin' you de fac's.
Cose ole Pher'oh believed in slav'ry,
　　But de Lawd he let him see,
Dat de people he put bref in, —
　　Evah mothah's son was free.

An' dahs othahs thinks lak Pher'oh,
　　But dey calls de Scriptuah liar,
Fu' de Bible says "a servant
　　Is a worthy of his hire."
An' you caint git roun' nor thoo dat,
　　An' you cain't git ovah it,
Fu' whatevah place you git in,
　　Dis hyeah Bible too 'll fit.

So you see de Lawd's intention
　　Evah sence de worl' began,
Was dat His almighty freedom
　　Should belong to evah man,
But I think it would be bettah,
　　Ef I'd pause agin to say,
That I'm talkin' 'bout ouah freedom
　　In a Bibleistic way.

But de Moses is a comin,
　　An' he's comin, suah and fas'
We kin hyeah his feet a-trompin',
　　We kin hyeah his trumpit blas'.
But I want to wa'n you people,
　　Don't you git too brigity;
An' don't you git to braggin'
　　'Bout dese things, you wait an' see.

But when Moses wif his powah,
　　Comes an' sets us chillen free,
We will praise de gracious Mastah
　　Dat has gin us liberty;
An' we'll shout ouah halleluyahs,
　　On dat mighty reck'nin' day,
When we'se reco'nized ez citiz' —
　　Huh uh! Chillen let us pray!

WE WEAR THE MASK

We wear the mask that grins and lies,
It hides our cheeks and shades our eyes —
This debt we pay to human guile;
With torn and bleeding hearts we smile
And mouth with myriad subtleties.

Why should the world be over-wise,
In counting all our tears and sighs?
Nay, let them only see us, while
   We wear the mask.

We smile, but oh great Christ, our cries
To Thee from tortured souls arise.
We sing, but oh the clay is vile
Beneath our feet, and long the mile;
But let the world dream otherwise,
   We wear the mask!

WHEN MALINDY SINGS

G'way an' quit dat noise, Miss Lucy —
   Put dat music book away;
What's de use to keep on tryin'?
   Ef you practice twell you're gray,
You cain't sta't no notes a-flyin'
   Like de ones dat rants and rings
F'om de kitchen to de big woods
   When Malindy sings.

You ain't got de nachel o'gans
   Fu' to make de soun' come right,
You ain't got de tu'ns an' twistin's
   Fu' to make it sweet an' light.
Tell you one thing now, Miss Lucy,
   An' I'm tellin' you fu' true,
When hit comes to raal right singin',
   'Tain't no easy thing to do.

Easy 'nough fu' folks to hollah,
   Lookin' at de lines an' dots,
When dey ain't no one kin sence it,
   An' de chune comes in in spots;
But fu' real melojous music,
   Dat jes' strikes yo' hawt and clings,

Jes' you stan' an' listen wif me,
  When Malindy sings.

Ain't you nevah heerd Malindy?
  Blessed soul, take up de cross!
Look heah, ain't you jokin', honey?
  Well, you don't know what you los'.
Y'ought to heah dat gal a-wa'blin',
  Robins, la'ks an' all dem things,
Heish dey moufs an' hides dey faces
  When Malindy sings.

Fiddlin' man, jes' stop his fiddlin',
  Lay his fiddle on de she'f;
Mockin'-bird quit tryin' to whistle,
  'Cause he jes' so shamed hisse'f.
Folks a-playin' on de banjo,
  Draps dey fingahs on de strings —
Bless yo' soul — fu'gits to move 'em,
  When Malindy sings.

She jes' spreads huh mouf and hollahs,
  "Come to Jesus," twell you heah
Sinnahs' tremblin' steps and voices,
  Timid-like a-drawin' neah;
Den she tu'ns to "Rock of Ages,"
  Simply to de cross she clings,
An' you fin' yo' teahs a drappin',
  When Malindy sings.

Who dat says dat humble praises
  Wif de Master nevah counts?
Heish yo' mouf, I heah dat music,
  Ez hit rises up an' mounts —
Floatin' by de hills an' valleys,
  Way above dis buryin' sod,
Ez hit makes its way in glory
  To de very gates of God!

Oh, hits sweetah dan de music
  Of an edicated band;
And hits dearah dan de battle's
  Song o' triumph in de lan'.
It seems holier dan evenin'
  When de solemn chu'ch bell rings,

Ez I sit an' ca'mly listen
    While Malindy sings.

Towsah, stop dat ba'kin' heah me!
    Mandy, make dat chile keep still;
Don't you heah de echoes callin'
    F'om de valley to de hill.
Let me listen, I can heah it,
    Th'oo de bresh of angel's wings,
Sof' an' sweet, "Swing Low, Sweet Chariot,"
    Ez Malindy sings.

THE HAUNTED OAK

Pray why are you so bare, so bare,
    Oh, bough of the old oak-tree;
And why, when I go through the shade you throw,
    Runs a shudder over me?

My leaves were green as the best, I trow,
    And sap ran free in my veins,
But I saw in the moonlight dim and weird
    A guiltless victim's pains.

I bent me down to hear his sigh;
    I shook with his gurgling moan,
And I trembled sore when they rode away,
    And left him here alone.

They'd charged him with the old, old crime,
    And set him fast in jail:
Oh, why does the dog howl all night long,
    And why does the night wind wail?

He prayed his prayer and he swore his oath,
    And he raised his hand to the sky;
But the beat of hoofs smote on his ear,
    And the steady tread drew nigh.

Who is it rides by night, by night,
    Over the moonlit road?
And what is the spur that keeps the pace,
    What is the galling goad?

And now they beat at the prison door,
    "Ho, keeper, do not stay!

We are friends of him whom you hold within,
    And we fain would take him away

"From those who ride fast on our heels
    With mind to do him wrong;
They have no care for his innocence,
    And the rope they bear is long."

They have fooled the jailer with lying words,
    They have fooled the man with lies;
The bolts unbar, the locks are drawn,
    And the great door open flies.

Now they have taken him from the jail,
    And hard and fast they ride,
And the leader laughs low down in his throat,
    As they halt my trunk beside.

Oh, the judge, he wore a mask of black,
    And the doctor one of white,
And the minister, with his oldest son,
    Was curiously bedight.

Oh, foolish man, why weep you now?
    'Tis but a little space,
And the time will come when these shall dread
    The mem'ry of your face.

I feel the rope against my bark,
    And the weight of him in my grain,
I feel in the throe of his final woe
    The touch of my own last pain.

And never more shall leaves come forth
    On a bough that bears the ban;
I am burned with dread, I am dried and dead,
    From the curse of a guiltless man.

And ever the judge rides by, rides by
    And goes to hunt the deer,
And ever another rides his soul
    In the guise of a mortal fear.

And ever the man he rides me hard,
    And never a night stays he;
For I feel his curse as a haunted bough,
    On the trunk of a haunted tree.

THE POET

He sang of life, serenely sweet,
    With, now and then, a deeper note.
    From some high peak, nigh yet remote,
He voiced the world's absorbing beat.

He sang of love when earth was young,
    And Love, itself, was in his lays.
    But ah, the world, it turned to praise
A jingle in a broken tongue.

ANNE SPENCER [ANNIE BETHEL SCALES BANNISTER] (1882–1975)

Only about 50 of Spencer's poems appeared in periodicals and anthologies, but in the 1920s she won national attention for her poetry and the friendship of the most prominent black writers.

DUNBAR

Ah, how poets sing and die!
Make one song and Heaven takes it;
Have one heart and Beauty breaks it;
Chatterton, Shelley, Keats and I —
Ah, how poets sing and die!

WHITE THINGS

Most things are colorful things — the sky, earth, and sea.
    Black men are most men; but the white are free!
White things are rare things; so rare, so rare
They stole from out a silvered world — somewhere.
Finding earth-plains fair plains, save greenly grassed,
They strewed white feathers of cowardice, as they passed;
    The golden stars with lances fine
    The hills all red and darkened pine,
They blanched with their wand of power;
And turned the blood in a ruby rose
To a poor white poppy-flower.

LETTER TO MY SISTER

It is dangerous for a woman to defy the gods;
To taunt them with the tongue's thin tip,
Or strut in the weakness of mere humanity,
Or draw a line daring them to cross;
The gods own the searing lightning,
The drowning waters, tormenting fears
And anger of red sins.

Oh, but worse still if you mince timidly —
Dodge this way or that, or kneel or pray,
Be kind, or sweat agony drops
Or lay your quick body over your feeble young;
If you have beauty or none, if celibate
Or vowed — the gods are Juggernaut,
Passing over . . . over . . .

This you may do:
Lock your heart, then, quietly,
And lest they peer within,
Light no lamp when dark comes down
Raise no shade for sun;
Breathless must your breath come through
If you'd die and dare deny
The gods their god-like fun.

CLAUDE McKAY (1890–1948)

A native of Jamaica, McKay traveled widely throughout the world. In several volumes of verse, four novels, an autobiography and a history of Harlem, he affirmed black identity and culture.

THE HARLEM DANCER

Applauding youths laughed with young prostitutes
And watched her perfect, half-clothed body sway;
Her voice was like the sound of blended flutes
Blown by black players upon a picnic day.
She sang and danced on gracefully and calm,
The light gauze hanging loose about her form;
To me she seemed a proudly-swaying palm

Grown lovelier for passing through a storm.
Upon her swarthy neck black, shiny curls
Profusely fell; and, tossing coins in praise,
The wine-flushed, bold-eyed boys, and even the girls,
Devoured her with their eager, passionate gaze;
But looking at her falsely-smiling face,
I knew her self was not in that strange place.

IF WE MUST DIE

If we must die — let it not be like hogs
Hunted and penned in an inglorious spot,
While round us bark the mad and hungry dogs,
Making their mock at our accursed lot.
If we must die — oh, let us nobly die,
So that our precious blood may not be shed
In vain; then even the monsters we defy
Shall be constrained to honor us though dead!
Oh, Kinsmen! We must meet the common foe;
Though far outnumbered, let us show us brave,
And for their thousand blows deal one death-blow!
What though before us lies the open grave?
Like men we'll face the murderous, cowardly pack,
Pressed to the wall, dying, but fighting back!

FLAME-HEART

So much I have forgotten in ten years,
So much in ten brief years! I have forgot
What time the purple apples come to juice,
And what month brings the shy forget-me-not.
I have forgot the special, startling season
Of the pimento's flowering and fruiting;
What time of year the ground doves brown the fields
And fill the noonday with their curious fluting.
I have forgotten much, but still remember
The poinsettia's red, blood-red, in warm December.

I still recall the honey-fever grass,
But cannot recollect the high days when
We rooted them out of the ping-wing path
To stop the mad bees in the rabbit pen.

I often try to think in what sweet month
The languid painted ladies used to dapple
The yellow by-road mazing from the main,
Sweet with the golden threads of the rose-apple.
I have forgotten — strange — but quite remember
The poinsettia's red, blood-red, in warm December.

What weeks, what months, what time of the mild year
We cheated school to have our fling at tops?
What days our wine-thrilled bodies pulsed with joy
Feasting upon blackberries in the copse?
Oh some I know! I have embalmed the days,
Even the sacred moments when we played,
All innocent of passion, uncorrupt,
At noon and evening in the flame-heart's shade.
We were so happy, happy, I remember,
Beneath the poinsettia's red in warm December.

THE TROPICS IN NEW YORK

Bananas ripe and green, and gingerroot,
        Cocoa in pods and alligator pears,
And tangerines and mangoes and grapefruit,
        Fit for the highest prize at parish fairs,

Set in the window, bringing memories
        Of fruit trees laden by low-singing rills,
And dewy dawns, and mystical blue skies
        In benediction over nunlike hills.

My eyes grew dim, and I could no more gaze;
        A wave of longing through my body swept,
And, hungry for the old, familiar ways,
        I turned aside and bowed my head and wept.

ENSLAVED

Oh when I think of my long-suffering race,
For weary centuries, despised, oppressed
Enslaved and lynched, denied a human place
In the great life line of the Christian West;
And in the Black Land disinherited,
Robbed in the ancient country of its birth,
My heart grows sick with hate, becomes as lead,

For this my race that has no home on earth.
Then from the dark depth of my soul I cry
To the avenging angel to consume
The white man's world of wonders utterly:
Let it be swallowed up in the earth's vast womb,
Or upward roll as sacrificial smoke
To liberate my people from its yoke!

JEAN TOOMER (1894–1967)

Toomer is best known for *Cane* (1923), a race-proud celebration of the rural South that combines lyrical fiction, drama and poetry in an unrivaled experimental form.

GEORGIA DUSK

The sky, lazily disdaining to pursue
    The setting sun, too indolent to hold
    A lengthened tournament for flashing gold,
Passively darkens for night's barbecue,

A feast of moon and men and barking hounds,
    An orgy for some genius of the South
    With blood-hot eyes and cane-lipped scented mouth,
Surprised in making folk-songs from soul sounds.

The sawmill blows its whistle, buzz-saws stop,
    And silence breaks the bud of knoll and hill,
    Soft settling pollen where plowed lands fulfill
Their early promise of a bumper crop.

Smoke from the pyramidal sawdust pile
    Curls up, blue ghosts of trees, tarrying low
    Where only chips and stumps are left to show
The solid proof of former domicile.

Meanwhile, the men, with vestiges of pomp,
    Race memories of king and caravan,
    High-priests, an ostrich, and a juju-man,
Go singing through the footpaths of the swamp.

Their voices rise . . the pine trees are guitars,
    Strumming, pine-needles fall like sheets of rain . .

Their voices rise . . the chorus of the cane
Is caroling a vesper to the stars. .

O singers, resinous and soft your songs
  Above the sacred whisper of the pines,
  Give virgin lips to cornfield concubines,
Bring dreams of Christ to dusky cane-lipped throngs.

HER LIPS ARE COPPER WIRE

whisper of yellow globes
gleaming on lamp-posts that sway
like bootleg licker drinkers in the fog

and let your breath be moist against me
like bright beads on yellow globes

telephone the power-house
that the main wires are insulate

(her words play softly up and down
dewy corridors of billboards)

then with your tongue remove the tape
and press your lips to mine
till they are incandescent

LANGSTON HUGHES (1902–1967)

For four decades, from 1926, the "Poet Laureate of Harlem" was the most prolific and popular African-American writer; he produced 13 volumes of poetry and many collections of fiction, drama, essays, history and autobiography.

THE NEGRO SPEAKS OF RIVERS

I've known rivers:
I've known rivers ancient as the world and older than the flow of human
    blood in human veins.

My soul has grown deep like the rivers.

I bathed in the Euphrates when dawns were young.
I built my hut near the Congo and it lulled me to sleep.

I looked upon the Nile and raised the pyramids above it.
I heard the singing of the Mississippi when Abe Lincoln went down
   to New Orleans, and I've seen its muddy bosom turn all golden in
   the sunset.

I've known rivers:
Ancient, dusky rivers.

My soul has grown deep like rivers.

JAZZONIA

Oh, silver tree!
Oh, shining rivers of the soul!

In a Harlem cabaret
Six long-headed jazzers play.
A dancing girl whose eyes are bold
Lifts high a dress of silken gold.

Oh, singing tree!
Oh, shining rivers of the soul!

Were Eve's eyes
In the first garden
Just a bit too bold?
Was Cleopatra gorgeous
In a gown of gold?

Oh, shining tree!
Oh, silver rivers of the soul!

In a whirling cabaret
Six long-headed jazzers play.

I, TOO

I, too, sing America.

I am the darker brother.
They send me to eat in the kitchen
When company comes,
But I laugh,
And eat well,
And grow strong.

Tomorrow,
I'll be at the table
When company comes.
Nobody'll dare
Say to me,
"Eat in the kitchen,"
Then.

Besides,
They'll see how beautiful I am
And be ashamed —

I, too, am America.

BOUND NO'TH BLUES

Goin' down the road, Lawd,
Goin' down the road.
Down the road, Lawd,
Way, way down the road.
Got to find somebody
To help me carry this load.

Road's in front o' me,
Nothin' to do but walk.
Road's in front o' me,
Walk . . . an' walk . . . an' walk.
I'd like to meet a good friend
To come along an' talk.

Hates to be lonely,
Lawd, I hates to be sad.
Says I hates to be lonely,
Hates to be lonely an' sad,
But ever' friend you finds seems
Like they try to do you bad.

Road, road, road, O!
Road, road . . . road . . . road, road!
Road, road, road, O!
On the no'thern road.
These Mississippi towns ain't
Fit fer a hoppin' toad.

MOTHER TO SON

Well, son, I'll tell you:
Life for me ain't been no crystal stair.
It's had tacks in it,
And splinters,
And boards torn up,
And places with no carpet on the floor —
Bare.
But all the time
I'se been a-climbin' on,
And reachin' landin's,
And turnin' corners,
And sometimes goin' in the dark
Where there ain't been no light.
So boy, don't you turn back.
Don't you set down on the steps
'Cause you finds it's kinder hard.
Don't you fall now —
For I'se still goin', honey,
I'se still climbin',
And life for me ain't been no crystal stair.

COUNTEE CULLEN (1903–1946)

Educated at New York University and Harvard, Cullen taught French
in New York City. He won several literary awards for his poetry, which
appeared in major national periodicals and five collections.

YET DO I MARVEL

I doubt not God is good, well-meaning, kind,
And did He stoop to quibble could tell why
The little buried mole continues blind,
Why flesh that mirrors Him must some day die,
Make plain the reason tortured Tantalus
Is baited by the fickle fruit, declare
If merely brute caprice dooms Sisyphus
To struggle up a never-ending stair.
Inscrutable His ways are, and immune

To catechism by a mind too strewn
With petty cares to slightly understand
What awful brain compels His awful hand.
Yet do I marvel at this curious thing:
To make a poet black, and bid him sing!

TO JOHN KEATS, POET, AT SPRINGTIME

I cannot hold my peace, John Keats;
There never was a spring like this;
It is an echo, that repeats
My last year's song and next year's bliss.
I know, in spite of all men say
Of Beauty, you have felt her most.
Yea, even in your grave her way
Is laid. Poor, troubled, lyric ghost,
Spring never was so fair and dear
As Beauty makes her seem this year.

I cannot hold my peace, John Keats,
I am as helpless in the toil
Of Spring as any lamb that bleats
To feel the solid earth recoil
Beneath his puny legs. Spring beats
Her tocsin call to those who love her,
And lo! the dogwood petals cover
Her breast with drifts of snow, and sleek
White gulls fly screaming to her, and hover
About her shoulders, and kiss her cheek,
While white and purple lilacs muster
A strength that bears them to a cluster
Of color and odor; for her sake
All things that slept are now awake.

And you and I, shall we lie still,
John Keats, while Beauty summons us?
Somehow I feel your sensitive will
Is pulsing up some tremulous
Sap road of a maple tree, whose leaves
Grow music as they grow, since your
Wild voice is in them, a harp that grieves
For life that opens death's dark door.
Though dust, your fingers still can push
The Vision Splendid to a birth,

Though now they work as grass in the hush
Of the night on the broad sweet page of the earth.

"John Keats is dead," they say, but I
Who hear your full insistent cry
In bud and blossom, leaf and tree,
Know John Keats still writes poetry.
And while my head is earthward bowed
To read new life sprung from your shroud,
Folks seeing me must think it strange
That merely spring should so derange
My mind. They do not know that you,
John Keats, keep revel with me, too.

FROM THE DARK TOWER

We shall not always plant while others reap
The golden increment of bursting fruit,
Not always countenance, abject and mute,
That lesser men should hold their brothers cheap;
Not everlastingly while others sleep
Shall we beguile their limbs with mellow flute,
Not always bend to some more subtle brute;
We were not made eternally to weep.

The night whose sable breast relieves the stark,
White stars is no less lovely being dark,
And there are buds that cannot bloom at all
In light, but crumple, piteous, and fall;
So in the dark we hide the heart that bleeds,
And wait, and tend our agonizing seeds.

ALPHABETICAL LIST OF TITLES

ALPHABETICAL LIST OF FIRST LINES

DOVER · THRIFT · EDITIONS

POETRY

LA VITA NUOVA, Dante Alighieri. 56pp. 0-486-41915-0

101 GREAT AMERICAN POEMS, The American Poetry & Literacy Project (ed.). (Available in U.S. only.) 96pp. 0-486-40158-8

ENGLISH ROMANTIC POETRY: An Anthology, Stanley Appelbaum (ed.). 256pp. 0-486-29282-7

BHAGAVADGITA, Bhagavadgita. 112pp. 0-486-27782-8

THE BOOK OF PSALMS, King James Bible. 128pp. 0-486-27541-8

IMAGIST POETRY: AN ANTHOLOGY, Bob Blaisdell (ed.). 176pp. (Available in U.S. only.) 0-486-40875-2

BLAKE'S SELECTED POEMS, William Blake. 96pp. 0-486-28517-0

SONGS OF INNOCENCE AND SONGS OF EXPERIENCE, William Blake. 64pp. 0-486-27051-3

THE CLASSIC TRADITION OF HAIKU: An Anthology, Faubion Bowers (ed.). 96pp. 0-486-29274-6

TO MY HUSBAND AND OTHER POEMS, Anne Bradstreet (Robert Hutchinson, ed.). 80pp. 0-486-41408-6

BEST POEMS OF THE BRONTË SISTERS (ed. by Candace Ward), Emily, Anne, and Charlotte Brontë. 64pp. 0-486-29529-X

SONNETS FROM THE PORTUGUESE AND OTHER POEMS, Elizabeth Barrett Browning. 64pp. 0-486-27052-1

MY LAST DUCHESS AND OTHER POEMS, Robert Browning. 128pp. 0-486-27783-6

POEMS AND SONGS, Robert Burns. 96pp. 0-486-26863-2

SELECTED POEMS, George Gordon, Lord Byron. 112pp. 0-486-27784-4

JABBERWOCKY AND OTHER POEMS, Lewis Carroll. 64pp. 0-486-41582-1

SELECTED CANTERBURY TALES, Geoffrey Chaucer. 144pp. 0-486-28241-4

THE RIME OF THE ANCIENT MARINER AND OTHER POEMS, Samuel Taylor Coleridge. 80pp. 0-486-27266-4

THE CAVALIER POETS: An Anthology, Thomas Crofts (ed.). 80pp. 0-486-28766-1

SELECTED POEMS, Emily Dickinson. 64pp. 0-486-26466-1

SELECTED POEMS, John Donne. 96pp. 0-486-27788-7

SELECTED POEMS, Paul Laurence Dunbar. 80pp. 0-486-29980-5

"THE WASTE LAND" AND OTHER POEMS, T. S. Eliot. 64pp. (Available in U.S. only.) 0-486-40061-1

THE RUBÁIYÁT OF OMAR KHAYYÁM: FIRST AND FIFTH EDITIONS, Edward FitzGerald. 64pp. 0-486-26467-X

A BOY'S WILL AND NORTH OF BOSTON, Robert Frost. 112pp. (Available in U.S. only.) 0-486-26866-7

THE ROAD NOT TAKEN AND OTHER POEMS, Robert Frost. 64pp. (Available in U.S. only.) 0-486-27550-7

THE GARDEN OF HEAVEN: POEMS OF HAFIZ, Hafiz. 112pp. 0-486-43161-4

HARDY'S SELECTED POEMS, Thomas Hardy. 80pp. 0-486-28753-X

A SHROPSHIRE LAD, A. E. Housman. 64pp. 0-486-26468-8

LYRIC POEMS, John Keats. 80pp. 0-486-26871-3

GUNGA DIN AND OTHER FAVORITE POEMS, Rudyard Kipling. 80pp. 0-486-26471-8

SNAKE AND OTHER POEMS, D. H. Lawrence. 64pp. 0-486-40647-4

DOVER·THRIFT·EDITIONS

POETRY

THE CONGO AND OTHER POEMS, Vachel Lindsay. 96pp. 0-486-27272-9

EVANGELINE AND OTHER POEMS, Henry Wadsworth Longfellow. 64pp. 0-486-28255-4

FAVORITE POEMS, Henry Wadsworth Longfellow. 96pp. 0-486-27273-7

"TO HIS COY MISTRESS" AND OTHER POEMS, Andrew Marvell. 64pp. 0-486-29544-3

SPOON RIVER ANTHOLOGY, Edgar Lee Masters. 144pp. 0-486-27275-3

SELECTED POEMS, Claude McKay. 80pp. 0-486-40876-0

RENASCENCE AND OTHER POEMS, Edna St. Vincent Millay. 64pp. (Not available in Europe or the United Kingdom) 0-486-26873-X

SELECTED POEMS, John Milton. 128pp. 0-486-27554-X

CIVIL WAR POETRY: An Anthology, Paul Negri (ed.). 128pp. 0-486-29883-3

ENGLISH VICTORIAN POETRY: AN ANTHOLOGY, Paul Negri (ed.). 256pp. 0-486-40425-0

GREAT SONNETS, Paul Negri (ed.). 96pp. 0-486-28052-7

THE RAVEN AND OTHER FAVORITE POEMS, Edgar Allan Poe. 64pp. 0-486-26685-0

ESSAY ON MAN AND OTHER POEMS, Alexander Pope. 128pp. 0-486-28053-5

EARLY POEMS, Ezra Pound. 80pp. (Available in U.S. only.) 0-486-28745-9

GREAT POEMS BY AMERICAN WOMEN: An Anthology, Susan L. Rattiner (ed.). 224pp. (Available in U.S. only.) 0-486-40164-2

GOBLIN MARKET AND OTHER POEMS, Christina Rossetti. 64pp. 0-486-28055-1

CHICAGO POEMS, Carl Sandburg. 80pp. 0-486-28057-8

CORNHUSKERS, Carl Sandburg. 157pp. 0-486-41409-4

COMPLETE SONNETS, William Shakespeare. 80pp. 0-486-26686-9

SELECTED POEMS, Percy Bysshe Shelley. 128pp. 0-486-27558-2

AFRICAN-AMERICAN POETRY: An Anthology, 1773–1930, Joan R. Sherman (ed.). 96pp. 0-486-29604-0

100 BEST-LOVED POEMS, Philip Smith (ed.). 96pp. 0-486-28553-7

NATIVE AMERICAN SONGS AND POEMS: An Anthology, Brian Swann (ed.). 64pp. 0-486-29450-1

SELECTED POEMS, Alfred Lord Tennyson. 112pp. 0-486-27282-6

AENEID, Vergil (Publius Vergilius Maro). 256pp. 0-486-28749-1

CHRISTMAS CAROLS: COMPLETE VERSES, Shane Weller (ed.). 64pp. 0-486-27397-0

GREAT LOVE POEMS, Shane Weller (ed.). 128pp. 0-486-27284-2

CIVIL WAR POETRY AND PROSE, Walt Whitman. 96pp. 0-486-28507-3

SELECTED POEMS, Walt Whitman. 128pp. 0-486-26878-0

THE BALLAD OF READING GAOL AND OTHER POEMS, Oscar Wilde. 64pp. 0-486-27072-6

EARLY POEMS, William Carlos Williams. 64pp. (Available in U.S. only.) 0-486-29294-0

FAVORITE POEMS, William Wordsworth. 80pp. 0-486-27073-4

WORLD WAR ONE BRITISH POETS: Brooke, Owen, Sassoon, Rosenberg, and Others, Candace Ward (ed.). (Available in U.S. only.) 0-486-29568-0

EARLY POEMS, William Butler Yeats. 128pp. 0-486-27808-5

"EASTER, 1916" AND OTHER POEMS, William Butler Yeats. 80pp. (Not available in Europe or United Kingdom.) 0-486-29771-3

DOVER·THRIFT·EDITIONS

NONFICTION

NARRATIVE OF THE LIFE OF FREDERICK DOUGLASS, Frederick Douglass. 96pp. 0-486-28499-9

SELF-RELIANCE AND OTHER ESSAYS, Ralph Waldo Emerson. 128pp. 0-486-27790-9

THE LIFE OF OLAUDAH EQUIANO, OR GUSTAVUS VASSA, THE AFRICAN, Olaudah Equiano. 192pp. 0-486-40661-X

THE AUTOBIOGRAPHY OF BENJAMIN FRANKLIN, Benjamin Franklin. 144pp. 0-486-29073-5

TOTEM AND TABOO, Sigmund Freud. 176pp. (Not available in Europe or United Kingdom.) 0-486-40434-X

LOVE: A Book of Quotations, Herb Galewitz (ed.). 64pp. 0-486-40004-2

PRAGMATISM, William James. 128pp. 0-486-28270-8

THE STORY OF MY LIFE, Helen Keller. 80pp. 0-486-29249-5

TAO TE CHING, Lao Tze. 112pp. 0-486-29792-6

GREAT SPEECHES, Abraham Lincoln. 112pp. 0-486-26872-1

THE PRINCE, Niccolò Machiavelli. 80pp. 0-486-27274-5

THE SUBJECTION OF WOMEN, John Stuart Mill. 112pp. 0-486-29601-6

SELECTED ESSAYS, Michel de Montaigne. 96pp. 0-486-29109-X

UTOPIA, Sir Thomas More. 96pp. 0-486-29583-4

BEYOND GOOD AND EVIL: Prelude to a Philosophy of the Future, Friedrich Nietzsche. 176pp. 0-486-29868-X

THE BIRTH OF TRAGEDY, Friedrich Nietzsche. 96pp. 0-486-28515-4

COMMON SENSE, Thomas Paine. 64pp. 0-486-29602-4

SYMPOSIUM AND PHAEDRUS, Plato. 96pp. 0-486-27798-4

THE TRIAL AND DEATH OF SOCRATES: Four Dialogues, Plato. 128pp. 0-486-27066-1

A MODEST PROPOSAL AND OTHER SATIRICAL WORKS, Jonathan Swift. 64pp. 0-486-28759-9

CIVIL DISOBEDIENCE AND OTHER ESSAYS, Henry David Thoreau. 96pp. 0-486-27563-9

WALDEN; OR, LIFE IN THE WOODS, Henry David Thoreau. 224pp. 0-486-28495-6

NARRATIVE OF SOJOURNER TRUTH, Sojourner Truth. 80pp. 0-486-29899-X

THE THEORY OF THE LEISURE CLASS, Thorstein Veblen. 256pp. 0-486-28062-4

DE PROFUNDIS, Oscar Wilde. 64pp. 0-486-29308-4

OSCAR WILDE'S WIT AND WISDOM: A Book of Quotations, Oscar Wilde. 64pp. 0-486-40146-4

UP FROM SLAVERY, Booker T. Washington. 160pp. 0-486-28738-6

A VINDICATION OF THE RIGHTS OF WOMAN, Mary Wollstonecraft. 224pp. 0-486-29036-0

All books complete and unabridged. All 5³⁄₁₆" x 8¼", paperbound. Available at your book dealer, online at **www.doverpublications.com**, or by writing to Dept. GI, Dover Publications, Inc., 31 East 2nd Street, Mineola, NY 11501. For current price information or for free catalogs (please indicate field of interest), write to Dover Publications or log on to **www.doverpublications.com** and see every Dover book in print. Dover publishes more than 500 books each year on science, elementary and advanced mathematics, biology, music, art, literary history, social sciences, and other areas.